Published by Spherical Publications

Copyright © 2014 Anand Deshpande

Anand Deshpande has asserted his
right under the Copyright, Designs and
Patents Act 1988 to be identified
as the author of this work.

ISBN 978-1-50529-706-5

Also available as a Kindle ebook
ISBN 978-1-84396-246-5

A CIP catalogue record for
this book is available from the
British Library.

Pre-press production
www.ebookversions.com

INDIA MY INDIA

501 Quiz Questions, Answers, and Explanations

ANAND DESHPANDE

SPHERICAL PUBLICATIONS

QUESTIONS

1 India is a vast country with an area of about 3.2 million km^2. In area, how many countries in the world are larger than India?

(a) six (b) three (c) two

2 How many states are in the Indian republic?

(a) 31 (b) 29 (c) 23

3 How many union territories are in India?

(a) seven (b) six (c) five

4 Amongst the states which is the smallest state in area?

(a) Goa (b) Manipur (c) Sikkim

5 Which is the longest river in India?

(a) Sindhu (b) Ganga (c) Brahmaputra

6 Considering the area, which is the largest state in India?

(a) Madhya Pradesh (b) Uttar Pradesh (c) Rajasthan

7 Which of the following rivers
flows from east to west to join the sea?

(a) Narmada (b) Kaveri (c) Godavari

8 What is the lowest latitude of mainland India?

(a) 8 degrees north
(b) 11 degrees north (c) 13 degrees north

9 Which is the least populous state in India?

(a) Sikkim (b) Nagaland (c) Manipur

10 The local time on this longitude is the
Indian Standard Time. Which is the longitude?

(a) 75^0 East (b) 82.5^0 East (c) 90^0 East

11 Which of the following cities
is on the 82.5^0 East longitude?

(a) New Delhi (b) Mirzapur (c) Bengaluru

12 Which is the most populated city in India?

(a) New Delhi (b) Kolkata (c) Mumbai

13 The river Brahmaputra flows into India.
Where does it originate?

(a) Manas sarovar (b) Kedarnath (c) Gangotri

14 Brahmaputra river flows from Tibet into India.
What is it called in Tibet?

(a) Yarlung-Tsangpo (b) Kosi (c) Padma

15 Thar desert is a feature of which state?

(a) Gujarat (b) Rajasthan (c) Haryana

16 Approximately what is the total length of
Brahmaputra river?

(a) 1400 km (b) 2900 km (c) 3500 km.

17 On which river in India was the
first hydroelectric power plant built?

(a) Kaveri in Karnataka
(b) Mahanadi in Odisha (c) Yamuna in Uttar Pradesh

18 Which of the following
is the tallest dam across a river?

(a) Krishnarajasagar across Kaveri
(b) Bhakra dam across Sutlaj
(c) Tehri dam across Bhagirathi

19 The name of this state means
"Land of the hill people". Which is it?

(a) Nagaland (b) Mizoram (c) Sikkim

20 Dudhsagar waterfall (Sea of milk) is a famous waterfall. Where can you find it?

(a) Goa (b) Uttarakhand (c) Bihar

21 Which of the following was a Union territory of the Republic of India since 1961 but was created a state in 1987?

(a) Meghalaya (b) Goa (c) Sikkim

22 How many states in India have a coastal line?

(a) Seven (b) Nine (c) Eleven

23 From west to east what is the maximum distance of Indian borders?

(a) 2900 kilometres
(b) 1600 kilometres (c) 1000 kilometres

24 Which state in India has the longest coastal line?

(a) Karnataka (b) Gujarat (c) West Bengal

25 From south to north borders of India what is the approximate distance?

(a) 1500 km (b) 2600 km (c) 3210 km

26 Aravalli is a mountain range. Where can you find it?

(a) Rajasthan (b) Kerala (c) Lakshadweep islands

27 Approximately what is the length
of the common land border of India with her
neighbours?

(a) 16,000 km (b) 10,000 km (c) 5,000 km

28 Guhar Moti is a small village
in Gujarat. What is its claim to fame?

(a) Birth place of Mahatma Gandhi
(b) The western-most inhabited place in India
(c) The least rainfall village in India

29 Radcliffe Line – what is it ?

(a) Demarcation line between Pakistan and India
(b) Demarcation line between Kashmir and China
(c) Demarcation line between India and Bangladesh

30 What is McMahon line?

(a) Boundary between India and China
(b) Boundary between India and Burma
(c) Boundary between India and Bangladesh

31 Cherrapunji is said to be the world's
wettest place with highest average rainfall.
Where is it?

(a) Assam (b) Arunachal Pradesh (c) Meghalaya

32 Which of the following modern states contains the ancient region described in the scriptures as Indrakil (Garden of Indra)?

(a) Kashmir (b) Gujarat (c) Sikkim

33 Nepal is a landlocked country sharing a common border with India. How long is the common border between India and Nepal?

(a) 1750 km (b) 1000 km (c) 650 km

34 Himalaya is one of the longest mountain ranges, stretching from Jammu Kashmir to Arunachal Pradesh. What is its approximate length?

(a) 2500 km (b) 1500 km (c) 1000 km

35 Sahyadri mountains are situated on the western coast in the south India. How long is this mountain range ?

(a) 1,600 km (b) 1000 km (c) 500 km

36 Itanagar is the capital of which of the following states?

(a) Gujarat (b) Haryana (c) Arunachal Pradesh

37 Which is the eastern-most state in India?

(a) Assam (b) Arunachal Pradesh (c) Mizoram

38 Which is the highest peak in India?

(a) Mt. Everest (b) Kangchenjunga (c) Nanda Devi

39 What is the capital of the union territory Dadra and Nagar Haveli?

(a) Silvassa (b) Panji (c) Dadra

40 Palk strait – where is it?

(a) Between Gujarat and Pakistan
(b) Between West Bengal and Bangladesh
(c) Between Tamil Nadu and Sri Lanka

41 The longest river Ganga flows into Bangladesh before ending in the bay of Bengal. Before entering into Bangladesh it divides. The distributary in Bangladesh is called Padma river. What is the distributary called in the Indian state West Bengal?

(a) Bhagirathi (b) Bhogavati (c) Bhagyavati

42 This river had a nickname "sorrow of Bengal" because of its frequent floods and destruction. Which one is it?

(a) Brahmaputra (b) Damodar (c) Ganga

43 The famous hill resort Darjeeling has given its name to a type of tea. Where is Darjeeling?

(a) Assam (b) West Bengal (c) Arunachal Pradesh

44 Ganga river is the longest river in India, at about 2600 km long. In how many states of India does it flow?

(a) Five (b) Three (c) Nine

45 Which is the tallest single tier waterfall in India?

(a) Dudhsagar (b) Jog (c) Nohkalikai

46 The union territory of Daman and Diu are to the south of Gujarat and west of Maharashtra. Daman and Diu are separated from each other by how many kilometres?

(a) 6 kilometres (b) 60 kilometres (c) 600 kilometres

47 Arunachal Pradesh, Meghalaya, Assam, Nagaland, Manipur, Mizoram and Tripura are collectively known as what?

(a) Minor States
(b) Eastern Estates (c) Seven –Sister States

48 After Ganga, which is the next longest river of India?

(a) Godavari (b) Yamuna (c) Mahanadi

49 Punjab gets its name because of the five rivers

in the area. (Five waters) Jhelum, Chenab,
Beas and Ravi are four of the five rivers. Which of
the following is the fifth river giving the name
to the geographical area?

(a) Sharayu (b) Sutlaj (c) Sindhu

50 In the region of the Punjab there existed
a river in the 5th century BCE but is non- existent
now. What was this now dried up river called?

(a) Saraswati (b) Lakshmi (c) Parvati

51 Nilgiri mountains can be found
in which of the following states?

(a) Karnataka (b) Arunachal Pradesh (c) Odisha

52 In which of the following states
can we see the Karakoram mountains?

(a) Kashmir (b) Rajasthan (c) Mizoram

53 Many invaders came to India through
the Khyber pass. Where is the Khyber pass?

(a) Pakistan-Afghanistan (b) Tibet (c) Myanmar

54 Which Indian state has common border with most
number of states?

(a) Madhya Pradesh (b) Assam (c) Uttar Pradesh

55 What is the meaning of the name
Kanchenjunga, the highest peak in India?

(a) Golden Shrine (b) Five Treasure Houses of Great Snow
(c) Abode of the gods

56 Kolkata is situated on the following river. Which one?

(a)Hooghly (b) Ganga (c) Padma

57 Howrah bridge is a famous
bridge across this river. Name the river.

(a) Hooghly (b) Ganga (c) Sutlaj

58 How many countries have common border with India?

(a) Nine (b) Seven (c) Five

59 How many states of India have
a common border with a country?

(a) 17 states (b) 10 states (c) 7 states

60 The tropic of cancer is the 23.5^0 north latitude.
It passes through how many states of India?

(a) Six (b) Eight (c) Nine

61 The meridian 82.5^0 East determines the
Indian Standard Time (IST). In how many states does
this meridian pass through?

(a)Five states (b) Three states (c) Two states

62 This Indian river was known as Hydaspes in
Greek in ancient times. Alexander the Great won his
battle on its banks against the Indian king.
By what name do we call this river?

(a) Sindhu (b) Sutlaj (c) Jhelum

63 Kamarupa was a famous ancient
kingdom, in which of the following modern regions?

(a) Kashmir (b) Assam (c) Karnataka

64 Pondicherry is renamed Puducherry. What is
the meaning of the word Puducherry in Tamil?

(a) Seashore (b) Religious Place (c) New Town

65 Andaman and Nicobar islands in the bay of Bengal
form a union territory of India. Approximately how
many islands form this union territory?

(a) 70 islands (b) 170 islands (c) 570 islands

66 Most of the Indian rivers run from west to the
east and join the bay of Bengal. Tapati and Narmada run
from east to west. Which of the following rivers
also runs from east to west?

(a) Mahi river (b) Mahanadi (c) Krishna river

67 India's gold source comes mostly from which state?

(a) Rajasthan (b) Karnataka (c) Kerala

68 The diamond mines of India are mostly

located in which state?

(a) Andhra Pradesh (b) Gujarat (c) Assam

69 This ancient famous city is on the banks
of the river Shipra. Which city is it?

(a) Varanasi (b) Kanchi (c) Ujjayini

70 Hindu Kush mountains are situated
in which of the following regions?

(a) Pakistan (b) Assam (c) Kashmir

71 Ganga river flows through Bangladesh
to join the Bay of Bengal. Which river does it
join in Bangladesh?

(a) Padma (b) Hooghly (c) Brahmaputra

72 What is the capital of Mizoram?

(a) Shillong (b) Kohima (c) Aizawl

73 Which is the largest freshwater lake in India?

(a)Kolleru in Andhra Pradsesh
(b) Wular in Kashmir (c) Dal in Kashmir

74 Kavaratti is the capital of

(a) Lakshadweep islands (b) Nagaland (c) Tripura

75 Kashmir is said to have got its name after an ancient
Hindu sage. Who was the sage?

(a) Kashyapa (b) Kausika (c) Kapila

76 Where is the southern-most tip of mainland India?

(a) Rameshwar (b) Kanyakumari (c) Dhanushkodi

77 Ten degrees channel. Where is it?

(a) Between Andaman and Nicobar islands
(b) Between India and Sri Lanka (c) between Lakshadweep
and Kerala

78 What is the National river of India?

(a) Yamuna (b) Ganga (c) Godavari

79 Saddle peak is the highest
mountain in this part of India. Where?

(a) Andaman islands (b) Lakshadweep islands (c) Goa

80 Indira Point is named after the Prime Minister
of India. Where is it?

(a) Southern-most tip of Nicobar island (b) Highest point in
Shimla (c) Northern-most place in Kashmir

81 Sindhu river flows from India into Pakistan
and ends in the Arabian sea. Where does it originate?

(a) Near Manas sarovar (b) Badarinath (c) Kedarnath

82 Which river of India has the longest earthen dam across
it?

(a) Narmada in Maharashtra (b) Mahanadi in Odisha
(c) Tungabhadra in Karnataka

83 Which state in India has the highest number of rivers?

(a) Andhra Pradesh (b) Maharashtra (c) Madhya Pradesh

84 Which river is called the Ganga ofthe South?

(a) Krishna (b) Kaveri (c) Tungabhadra

85 Which state in India has the common
border with least number of states?

(a) Goa (b) Kashmir (c) Sikkim

86 Which is the most densely populated state in India?

(a) Goa (b) Kerala (c) Bihar

87 Who was the first Indian to climb the
highest mountain the Mount Everest?

(a) Avatar Singh Cheema (b) Tenzing Norgay
(c) Bachendri Pal

88 Kangchenjunga, the highest mountain
of India, is at the border of India and Nepal. The
second highest mountain Nanda Devi is
entirely in India. Where is it?

(a) Uttarakhand (b) Kashmir (c) Arunachal Pradesh

89 Which state in India has the least number of rivers?

(a) Bihar (b) Kerala (c) Haryana

90 Indus valley civilization flourished before
the Aryans arrived in India. What period of time
was this civilization?

(a) 2500 - 1500 BCE (b) 50,000 – 25,000 BCE (c) 1st
century BCE

91 Scholars believe that our ancestors, the Aryans,
migrated to India from Asia Minor. In modern geography
where would that area be?

(a) Western Turkey (b) Afghanistan (c) Manchuria

92 Harappa and Mohenjodaro are the famous
ancient cities of Indus Valley civilization. Where are their
ruins situated in modern geography?

(a) Afghanistan (b) Pakistan (c) Iran

93 Which of the following Indian towns
has also shown the ruins of the Indus Valley
civilization?

(a) Kalibangan (b) Udaipur (c) Ajmer

94 What is the meaning of the name
Mohenjodaro – the place famous for its ruins of
the Indus valley civilization?

(a) River valley (b) Mound of the dead (c) Ancient town

95 How did Bharatavarsha or Bharata
Desha get its anglicized name India?

(a) Greek language (b) German (c) Arabic

96 The famous battle of Hydaspes (on the banks
of the river Jhelum) was against the invading Greeks. Who
was the Indian king opposing the invader?

(a) Chandragupta Maurya (b) Porus (c) King Bimbisara

97 Alexander the Great invaded India in 326 BC.
How much of India did he occupy?

(a) Region of the Jhelum river (b) Up to Delhi
(c) Up to Varanasi

98 Chandragupta established the Mauryan Empire in 321
BCE. When did this dynasty end?

(a) CE 321 (b) 185 BCE (c) 232 BCE

99 Emperor Ashoka annexed the Kalinga
kingdom to his vast empire in the third century BCE
after his victorious bloody battle. Where in
modern regions was the Kalinga kingdom?

(a) Karnataka (b) Gujarat (c) Odisha

100 Bimbisara was the monarch who ruled in
the second half of the 6th century BCE. Where was
his kingdom?

(a) Saurashtra (b) Magadha (c) Kashmir

101 The ancient kingdom of Magadha
once had its capital at the following city.

(a) Varanasi (b) Rajagriha (c) Ujjayini

102 Who was the father of Ashoka,
the Emperor of Magadha?

(a) Chandragupta (b) Bindusara (c) Ajatashatru

103 This Greek ambassador to the Mauryan
court in the 3rd century BCE has provided many
of his observations of the Indian society
at the time. Who was he?

(a) Megasthenes (b) Herodotus (c) Seleucus

104 Some part of Afghanistan was part
of the Indian empire in ancient time. Who was
the Indian monarch at the time?

(a) King Ashoka (b) King Ajatashatru
(c) King Harshavardhana

105 The Mauryan kings had built a Royal
Highway connecting which two cities?

(a) Pataliputra - Takshashila (b) Pataliputra- Ujjayini
(c) Pataliputra - Varanasi

106 Kharavela was a famous king in
the first century CE. Where in modern India was
the capital of his vast empire?

(a) Kerala (b) Kashmir (c) Odisha

107 The Hindu epic the Mahabharata describes
the battle of Kurukshetra. Where was the battlefield of
Kurukshetra in relation to modern India?

(a) Near Patna (b) Near Kashi (Benares) (c) Near Delhi

108 In the first century BCE the powerful dynasty of
Shatavahana arose. It was also called by what other name?

(a) Kalinga dynasty (b) Andhra dynasty (c) Chola dynasty

109 The ancient city Pratishthana was the
capital of the Shatavahana kingdom. Where would
we find this capital city in modern India?

(a) Andhra Pradesh((b) Maharashtra (c) Karnataka

110 The Gupta dynasty began in CE 321.
Who was the first king of this illustrious dynasty?

(a) Chandragupta (b) Samudragupta (c) Skandagupta

111 The Gupta dynasty had Chandragupta II
(CE375 - 415). By what name is he recognized in history?

(a) Anandvardhana (b) Vikramaditya (c) Ashvaghosha

112 Harshavardhana had a vast empire
in the north of India. He was defeated at the Narmada
river by this king in south India. Who was he?

(a)Pulikeshin II (b) Mayuravarma (c) Vishnuvardhana

113 Pulikeshin II defeated Harsha in the 7th century CE.
He was the Chalukya king. In modern geography,

where is Badami the capital of Pulikeshin II ?

(a) Andhra Pradesh (b) Karnataka (c) Tamil Nadu

114 Ghazni Mahmud invaded India for
the first time in CE 998. Where is Ghazni?

(a)Afghanistan (b) Turkey (c) Iran

115 Mahmud of Ghazni invaded India
from CE 998 onwards. How many times
did he invade India?

(a) 7 times (b) 10 times (c) 17times

116 The most famous Somanath temple
in Saurashtra was sacked by Ghazni Mahmud.
When was it?

(a) CE 1000 (b) CE 1009 (c) CE 1024

117 Who was the last Indian king whom
Ghuri Muhammad defeated in CE 1192
and occupied Delhi?

(a) Prithviraj Chauhan (b) Rana Pratapsingh (c) Jayapal

118 Who was the first Sultan of Delhi?

(a) Qutb - ud - din Aibak (b) Mohammadbin Tughlaq
(c) Ghuri Muhammad

119 Who founded the "Slave Dynasty" at Delhi in the 12th
century CE?

(a) Ghuri Muhammad (b) Qutb –ud- din Aibak
(c) Mohammadbin Tughlaq

120 Mohammad bin Tughlaq, the Sultan
of Delhi moved his capital from Delhi to Daulatabad.
By what name was Daulatabad known before?

(a) Devagiri (b) Dhanapuri (c) Dharmapuri

121 In CE 1336 this Hindu dynasty was
established in south India by two brothers called
Hakka and Bukka. Name that dynasty.

(a) Hoysala dynasty (b) Vijayanagar dynasty
(c) Pandya dynasty

122 This vast South Indian kingdom broke
into five smaller kingdoms of Ahmednagar, Bijapur,
Bidar, Berar, and Golconda kingdoms.
What was this kingdom?

(a) Bahamani kingdom (b) Vijayangara kingdom
(c) Hoysala kingdom

123 The Portuguese explorer Vasco da Gama
sailed to India for the first time and landed at
Calicut. When was it?

(a) CE 1600 (b) CE 1565 (c) CE 1498

124 Where is Calicut?

(a) Goa (b) Karnataka (c) Kerala

125 Which famous Italian navigator in the

fifteenth century tried unsuccessfully to find
the sea route from Europe to India?

(a) Amerigo Vespucci (b) Christopher Columbus
(c) Marco Polo

126 Who in CE 1510 captured Goa from the
Sultan of Bijapur and made it a Portuguese territory?

(a) Vasco da Gama (b) St. Francis Xavier
(c) Alphonso de Albuquerque

127 The first battle of Panipat was in CE 1526.
Babur won the battle and established the Mughal
rule in Delhi for the first time. Whom did he
defeat in this battle?

(a) Ibrahim Lodi (b) Sher Shah (c) Mohammad bin Tughlaq

128 Where in the modern Indian state
is the Panipat battleground situated?

(a) Uttar Pradesh (b) Punjab (c) Haryana

129 The first Mughal emperor of India was Babur.
What is the meaning of the name Babur?

(a) Lion (b) Elephant (c) Eagle

130 This Mughal emperor died when he fell
accidentally from the stairs in his palace. Who is it?

(a) Aurangzeb (b) Humayun (c) Jahangir

131 This Mughal Emperor was known as

Alamgir (world-seizer). Who was it?

(a) Babur (b) Aurangzeb (c) Akbar

132 Who was the last Mughal Emperor of India?

(a) Aurangzeb (b) Bahadur Shah II (c) Nasiruddin Shah

133 Babur was the first Mughal emperor of India.
How did the name Mughal come?

(a)Conqueror (b) Great and Grand (c) Mongol

134 Which Mughal king was defeated by
Sher Shah and ousted from Delhi? The fugitive Mughal
king returned after about fourteen years and
recaptured Delhi and became the king once again!

(a) Akbar (b) Jahangir (c) Humayun

135 He became the Mughal king
at the age of thirteen. Who was he?

(a) Akbar (b) Jahangir (c) Aurangzeb

136 Which Mughal emperor married a Hindu?
He married the daughter of a Rajput king.

(a)Humayun (b) Shah Jahan (c) Akbar

137 Prince Khurram became a Mughal emperor.
By what name is he better known?

(a) Shah Jahan (b) Humayun (c) Jahangir

138 This Mughal emperor was illiterate.
Who was the emperor?

(a) Babur (b) Humayun (c) Akbar

139 Devagiri was renamed as Daulatabad.
Who changed its original name?

(a) Mohammad bin Tughlaq (b) Aurangzeb (c) Shah Jahan

140 The Mughal emperor Akbar reigned
for how many years?

(a) 17 years (b) 29 years (c) 49 years

141 Who was the British ambassador to the
Mughal court during the time of Jahangir?

(a) Sir Thomas Roe (b) Sir Walter Raleigh
(c) Sir Francis Drake

142 Mumtaz Mahal was the beloved wife
of the Emperor Shah Jahan. She died during the
delivery of her baby. In all how many
pregnancies did she have?

(a)Four (b) Nine (c) Fourteen

143 Shah Jahan was imprisoned by his son
Aurangzeb for nearly eight years until his death in
captivity! Where was he kept a prisoner?

(a) Red Fort Delhi (b) Agra Fort
(c) Panch Mahal at Fatepur Sikri

144 Aurangzeb reigned for how many years?

(a) 29 years (b) 39 years (c) 49 years

145 The poll tax levied by the Mughal emperors on the Hindus was called Jazia (also spelt Jezia, Jaziyah) . One emperor abolished the Jazia on Hindus. Who was that?

(a) Aurangzeb (b) Akbar (c) Jahangir

146 Tansen was a famous singer and musician. In which Mughal emperor's court was he?

(a) Akbar (b) Shah Jahan (c) Jahangir

147 In Mughal Emperor Akbar's court, many Hindus held high posts. Todar Mal was one of them. What post did he hold?

(a) Finance Minister (b) Religious affairs (c) Defence

148 Akbar built a new city. What was it?

(a) Agra (b) Fatepur Sikri (c) Allahabad

149 Agra was the capital of Akbar's empire. Then he moved the capital to Fatepur Sikri for a while. From there he yet again moved the capital to which city?

(a) Lahore (b) Hyderabad (c) Delhi

150 Who re-introduced the Jaziyah (poll tax) on Hindus which was earlier abolished by Akbar?

(a) Jahangir (b) Shah Jahan (c) Aurangzeb

151 Which of the Mughal emperors reigned the longest?

(a) Babur (b) Akbar (c) Aurangzeb

152 The Peacock throne was a splendid throne with innumerable encrusted gemstones. Which Mughal emperor got it made?

(a) Akbar (b) Jahangir (c) Shah Jahan

153 Aurangzeb's son Bahadur Shah I was the seventh Mughal emperor. How many years did he reign?

(a) 23 years (b) 9 years (c) 5 years

154 Which historical figure in India had horses named Sarangi, Pavan and Badal?

(a) Jahangir (b) Hyder Ali (c) Queen Jhansi Lakshmibai

155 Shah Jahan built the Taj Mahal in memory of his wife Mumtaz Mahal. How many times did he marry?

(a)1 (b) 3 (c) 4

156 Taj Mahal is situated on the banks of a river. Name that river.

(a) Ganga (b) Kosi (c) Yamuna (Jamuna)

157 Marco Polo visited India in the 13th century CE. Which is his country of origin?

(a)Morocco (b) Poland (c) Italy

158 Niccolo de Conti from Venice visited India.
When did he visit?

(a) 15th century CE (b) 13th century CE (c) 9thcentury CE

159 Chinese traveller the Buddhist monk Fa-Hien
(Fa-Hsien) visited India and has written extensively about
India. When did he visit India?

(a) 2nd Century CE (b) 5th century CE (c) 12th century CE

160 Ibn Battuta was a traveller from Morocco.
When did he visit India?

(a) 14th century CE (b) 16th century CE (c) 18th century
CE

161 Babur's grandson Akbar was victorious
in the second battle of Panipat in CE1556.
Whom did he defeat in this battle?

(a)Hemu (b) Sher Shah (c) Uday Singh

162 The last and the third battle of Panipat
was fought between Ahmed Shah Durrani and the
Marathas.In which year?

(a) CE 1761 (b) CE 1799 (c) CE 1857

163 When the Mughal empire collapsed in the
18th century the ruler of Persia invaded India and
carried off the famous Peacock throne amongst
other loots. Who was this Persian ruler?

(a) Nadir Shah (b) Ahmed Shah Durrani (c) Adil Shah

164 The East India Company in England
was instrumental in establishing the British rule in India.
When was this trading company established?

(a) CE 1600 (b) CE 1757 (c) CE 1857

165 Tipu Sultan was the heroic king
in south India, who fought the British East India
company army in the famous Anglo-Mysore wars.
In the fourth Anglo-Mysore battle in 1799
he was defeated and killed.
By what famous soubriquet was he known?

(a) Lion of Mysore (b) Tiger of Mysore
(c) Cheetah of Mysore

166 The famous Ahilyabai Holkar ruled for
thirty years (CE 1765-1795) Where did she rule?

(a) Gwalior (b) Jaipur (c) Indore

167 Jhansi Lakshmibai fought against the British
and died in Gwalior (Madhya Pradesh). How old was she
when killed by the British?

(a) 29 years (b) 47 years (c) 55 years

168 The year 1857 is a historic year for India.
It was the year of Indian Rebellion against the British.
Where did it start?

(a) Meerut (b) Surat (c) New Delhi

169 The East India Company was initially a trading company founded in CE 1600 in London. The company led to the establishment of British rule in India until 1947. When did the East India Company dissolve?

(a) 1757 (b) 1858 (c) 1948

170 In which year did the Mughal rule in India end?

(a) CE 1858 (b) CE 1905 (c) CE 1799

171 Krishnadevaraya the king of Vijayanagar (CE 1471-1529) and Jhansi Lakshmibai (CE 1828-1858) were both afflicted by this deadly disease. Which disease?

(a) Polio (b) Malaria (c) Smallpox

172 This king of 16th century was a poet and wrote the famous work called Amuktamalyada. Who is the king?

(a) Krishnadevaraya (b) Harshavardhana (c) Vishnuvardhana

173 Ustad Ahmad Lahauri is known for what?

(a) Great Musician of Jahangir's court
(b) Great swordsman of Akbar
(c) Chief architect of the Taj Mahal at Agra

174 This famous woman in history married the king Bhoja Raja of Mewar. Who is she?

(a) Padmini (b) Meerabai (c) Jhansi Lakshmibai

175 Nur Jahan was the wife of this Mughal emperor.
Who was the emperor?

(a) Jahangir (b) Aurangzeb (c) Akbar

176 About 20,000 workers were needed
to build the Taj Mahal. How many years did it take to
complete the construction?

(a) 5 years (b) 11 years (c) 20 years

177 Prince Salim is known as the Mughal Emperor
Jahangir. He ascended the throne in CE 1605.What is the
meaning of his name Jahangir?

(a) World Conqueror (b) World Loving (c) World Citizen

178 Which Mughal emperor designed
the famous Shalimar gardens in Kashmir?

(a) Shah Jahan (b) Jahangir (c) Aurangzeb

179 She is credited with discovering a method
of extracting the scent from rose petals
(attar). Who is this Queen?

(a) MumtazMahal (b) Nur Jahan (c) Razia

180 The historic battle of Plassey led to the
British rule in India. When did this battle take place?

(a)CE 1757 (b) CE 1857 (c) CE 1761

181 During the British rule of India, some
Princely states were independent and were not subject to

direct British rule. In terms of geographical area of the whole country, what percentage of land was under the direct rule of British empire?

(a) 95% (b) 75% (c) 60%

182 Veerapandiya Kattabomman was an 18th-century king who fought against the British. He lost and was hanged by the British. Where did he have his kingdom?

(a) Tamil Nadu (b) Karnataka (c) Kerala

183 Queen Kittur Channamma fought the British. The Doctrine of Lapse was applied against her kingdom by the British. The British officer Thackarey was killed in the battle. Where was this illustrious Kittur Channamma a queen?

(a) Rajasthan (b) Karnataka (c) Tamil Nadu

184 Takshashila or Taxila was a city with a famous university in ancient India. Today it is in Pakistan. It was the capital of which ancient kingdom?

(a)Kashmir (b) Gandhar (c) Saurashtra

185 Like the city of Takshashila, the city of Nalanda was famous for its university in ancient times. The university was destroyed by Turkish raiders in the 12th century. Where in modern India is Nalanda city situated?

(a) Bihar (b) Uttar Pradesh (c) Haryana

186 Alakapuri was the name of this famous ancient city. What is it commonly known as?

(a) Ujjayini (b) Jagannathpuri (c) Dwaraka

187 Which Indian city was passed to Britain in CE 1662 by Portugal as part of dowry of Catherine of Braganza?

(a)Madras (Chennai) (b) Calcutta (Kolkata) (c) Bombay (Mumbai)

188 Puducherry (earlier Pondicherry) is a union territory. Before the independence of India it was Governed by whom?

(a) French (b) Portuguese (c) Dutch

189 This city is nicknamed "Pink City".Which one?

(a) Patna (b) Pinjore (c) Jaipur

190 India has sheltered for centuries the Parsees (also spelled Parsi) who fled Iran to escape the persecution by the Muslims. Where in India are they mostly settled?

(a) Jaipur (b) Mumbai (c) Thiruvananthapuram

191 Who was the founder of the Parsi (Parsee) religion?

(a) Confucius (b) Zoroaster (c) Moses

192 What is the sacred scripture of the Parsee religion called?

(a) Zaratushtra (b) Avesta (c) The Old Testament

193 Theravada is a division of which religion?

(a) Jainism (b) Judaism (c) Buddhism

194 What is the given name of the Buddha

(a)Maitreya (b) Devadatta (c) Siddhartha

195 Which king of the Magadha kingdom
was a contemporary of the Buddha?

(a) Bimbisara (b) Chandragupta (c) Ashoka

196 By what name is the Buddhist monastery known?

(a) Vihara (b) Nirvana (c) Mahayana

197 What is the name of the wife of the Buddha?

(a) Amrapali (b) Yashodhara (c) Mayadevi

198 What is the name of the only son of the Buddha?

(a) Devadatta (b) Rahul (c) Anand

199 In Sikhism it is said that the powers
of Guru now rest in the Khalsa. What is the meaning
of the word'Khalsa'?

(a) Pure or genuine (b) Forbidden (c) Ancestor

200 What is an agiary?

(a) Jain monastery (b) Jewish Temple
(c) Fire Temple of Parsees

201 In which language did the Buddha teach the people?

(a) Magadhi (b) Pali (c) Sanskrit

202 The Buddha is said to have attained
the enlightenment under the sacred Pipal tree after
he meditated. For how many days
did he meditate?

(a) 7 days (b) 17 days (c) 49 days

203 Siddhartha (the Buddha) abandoned his
home, family and began his search for the truth and
enlightenment. How old was he when he
started this spiritual search?

(a) 23 years (b) 30 years (c) 49 years

204 Siddhartha (later the Buddha) was born in Lumbini.
Where is Lumbini?

(a) Tibet (b) Nepal (c) Sikkim

205 What was the name of the horse of
Siddhartha (the Buddha)?It is said that the horse died
of sadness soon after the Buddha parted
with his horse.

(a) Katyayani (b) Kunjara (c) Kanthaka

206 A tooth of the Buddha is said to be
preserved in the holy place and displayed for public

viewing even today. Where is it now?

(a) Tokyo in Japan (b) Kathmandu in Nepal
(c) Kandy in Sri Lanka

207 After gaining the enlightenment the Buddha
gave his first sermon to his disciples at the Deer Park.
Where was this famous Deer Park?

(a) Sarnath (b) Kapilavastu (c) Lumbini

208 In Hindu sacred scriptures, there are four Vedas.
Which of the following is the oldest?

(a) Samaveda (b) Atharva Veda (c) Rig Veda

209 Which religious founder died in the year 527 BCE?

(a) Mahavira (b) The Buddha (c) Zaratushtra

210 This Christian saint is believed to have brought
Christianity to India in the 5th century CE. Who was it?

(a) St. Paul (b) St. Xavier (c) St. Thomas

211 Which famous Hindu philosopher was
born in the village Kaladi in Kerala?

(a) Shankaracharya (b) Patanjali (c) Kanada

212 Hinayana and Mahayana are divisions of which
religion?

(a) Buddhism (b) Jainism (c) Sikhism

213 The collection of over 500 Buddhist legends is known
by what name?

(a) Eightfold Path (b) Dhammapada (c) Jataka Stories

214 Which is the oldest of all the Hindu scriptures?

(a) Manu Smriti (b) Bhagavadgita (c) the Rig Veda

215 Svetambara and Digambara are two
main branches of this ancient religion. Name it.

(a) Lokayata (b) Jainism (c) Parsee (Parsi)

216 Yoga system of Hindu philosophy
was founded by whom?

(a) Patanjali (b) Panini (c) Chanakya

217 What name is given to the great monks
of Jain religion? Mahavira was the last one.

(a) Bhikku (b) Tirthankara (c) Tathagata

218 This Indian philosopher is regarded
as the greatest exponent of the *advaita* (non-duality)
philosophy and lived only 32 years. During
that brief life he travelled all over India and revived
Hinduism. Who was he?

(a) Ramanujacharya (b) Shankaracharya (c) Madhvacharya

219 What is the meaning of the word Islam?

(a) Submit to God
(b) I believe in God (c) I believe in the Prophet

220 The Koran is the holy scripture of Islam.
What is the meaning of the word Koran?

(a) Recital (b) One God (c) God is merciful

221 Siddhartha (later the Buddha) left his wife
and the only son to seek enlightenment. When he left
home at night who was his charioteer?

(a) Channa (b) Devadatta (c) Anand

222 Name the place where the Buddha died.

(a)Kushinagar (b) Jagannathpuri (c) Kapilavastu

223 Where was the famous tree under
which the Buddha attained enlightenment?

(a) Varanasi in Uttar Pradesh (b) Gaya in Bihar
(c) Shrinagar in Kashmir

224 The Buddha belonged to this ancient tribe. Which
tribe?

(a) Shakya (b) Shatavahana (c) Bhilla

225 Mahavira, the founder of the Jain religion
was born c 599 BCE. Where was he born?

(a)Vaishali (b) Shravana Belgola (c) Kapilavastu

226 By what name was Mahavira known in his childhood?

(a)Abhay (b) Akash (c) Vardhamana

227 Kumbh Mela at Haridwar in Uttarakhand
is a religious festival attracting millions of Hindu
pilgrims from all over the world. How
frequently is it celebrated?

(a)10 years (b) 12 years (c) 14 years

228 Apart from Haridwar,Kumbh Mela
is celebrated in three other holy places in India where,
according to Hindu mythology, drops of *amrit*
fell from the kumbha carried by the gods.
Prayag (now Allahabad) and Ujjayini are two places.
Which is the third one?

(a) Dwaraka (b) Jagannatahpuri (c) Nashik

229 In 1950s the Buddhist spiritual guru
the Dalai Lama fled Tibet with his followers and since
then made Dharmashala his head office.
Where in India is Dharmashala of the exiled Dalai Lama?

(a) Himachal Pradesh (b) Rajasthan (c) Sikkim

230 He was one of the great Hindu socio-
religious reformers in the 12th century in Karnataka.
His followers are shaivites. He was also the
minister of the Jain king Bijjala. Who was he?

(a) Basaveshvara (b) Jnanadeva (c) Somadev

231 This Mughal emperor started a new

religion called Din-ilahi. Name the emperor.

(a)Aurangzeb (b) Shah Jahan (c) Akbar

232 Tukaram (17th century CE) was a great Bhakti or devotional poet and saint. Where was he from?

(a) Rajasthan (b) Bihar (c) Maharashtra

233 Purandaradasa was a great poet and devotee in the sixteenth century. His innumerable philosophical, moralistic and devotional songs are very popular. Where is he from?

(a) Karnataka (b) Odisha (c) Tamil Nadu

234 Who founded the Sikh religion?

(a) Guru Gobindsingh (b) Guru Nanak (c) Guru Ramdas

235 Who was the last Guru of the Sikhs?

(a) Guru Arjan (b) Guru Gobindsingh (c) Guru Ramdas

236 Who compiled the Adi Granth, the sacred scriptures of the Sikh religion?

(a) Guru Arjan (b) Guru Gobindsingh (c) Guru Nanak

237 Which Sikh Guru created Khalsa or the brotherhood of Sikhs?

(a)Guru Gobindsingh (b) Guru Arjan (c) Guru Ramdas

238 Who built the Golden Temple of Amritsar?

(a) Guru Nanak (b) Guru Gobindsingh (c) Guru Arjan

239 How many Gurus are in the Sikh religion?
(a)Three (b) Ten (c) fifteen

240 Who in 1875 founded the Hindu
religious sect Arya Samaj?

(a) Vivekananda (b) Dayananda Saraswati
(c) Ram Mohan Roy

241 Who founded the Brahmo Samaj?

(a) Ram Mohan Roy (b) Ramakrishna Paramahamsa
(c) Vivekananda

242 Mosque (Masjid) is the holy place of the Muslims.
What is the meaning of the word Masjid?

(a) Meditation (b) Place of prostration and prayer
(c) Place of holy sermon

243 It was in 1893 Swami Vivekananda
represented India and achieved great honour for India
and Hinduism at the International Parliament
of Religions. In which city in America was this
conference held?

(a) New York (b) Chicago (c) Boston

244 Bengal came under the British rule following
the battle of Plassey. Who led the British in this battle,
which led to the beginning of British rule of India

for the next two hundred years.

(a) Lord Wellesley (b) William Bentinck (c) Robert Clive

245 English language became the official language and the business language in India during the rule of which of the following?

(a) William Bentinck (b) Lord Curzon (c) Lord Wellesley

246 The British sold Kashmir to the king of Jammu for Rs 75 lakhs. Who was the king of Jammu at the time?

(a) Karan Singh (b) Dulip Singh (c) Raja Gulabsingh

247 Who was the first Governor General of India?

(a) William Bentinck (b) Warren Hastings (c) Lord Mountbatten

248 Who was the first Viceroy of India?

(a) Lord Canning (b) William Bentinck (c) Lord Curzon

249 Who was the Viceroy of India when Bengal was divided in 1905 into predominantly Hindu and Muslim regions?

(a) Lord Wellesley (b) Lord Canning (c) Lord Curzon

250 Who was the British General responsible for the horrific Amritsar massacre?

(a) General Dyer (b) General Haig (c) General Wellesley

251 Who was the first Indian to be elected as
an MP (Member of Parliament) to the British Parliament
from a borough of London during the British
rule of India?
(a) Motilal Nehru (b) Gopal Krishna Gokhale
(c) Dadabhoy Naoroji

252 When was the Indian National Congress established?

(a) 1885 (b) 1901 (c) 1942

253 Who was called the Grand Old Man of India?

(a) Lokamanya Tilak (b) Mahatma Gandhi
(c) Dadabhoy Naoroji

254 When did Delhi become the
administrative centre of India?

(a) 1912 (b) 1937 (c) 1947

255 The British rule divided Bengal into
Hindu and Muslim regions of West and East Bengal.
However the Viceroy reversed this partition
and once again Bengal became a united region.
When was this partition reversed and Bengal
became a united region?

(a) 1911 (b) 1921 (c) 1931

256 Who was the Indian national leader to use for the first
time the word Swaraj (self-rule) for India's goal?

(a)Gopalkrishna Gokhale (b) Dadabhoy Naoroji
(c) Subhas Chandra Bose

257 Mohandas Karamachand Gandhi is known as Mahatma Gandhi. Who bestowed the honorific title " Mahatma"for the first time?
(a) Gopal Krishna Gokhale (b) Jawaharlal Nehru (c) Rabindranath Tagore

258 During the struggle for India's freedom, when was the Muslim League founded?

(a) 1885 (b) 1906 (c) 1942

259 Who founded the Servants of India Society?

(a) Mahatma Gandhi (b) Gopal Krishna Gokhale (c) Vinoba Bhave

260 Who was the freedom fighter famous for his saying "self-rule is my birth right"

(a) Subhas Chandra Bose (b) Lokamanya Tilak (c) Lala Lajapat Rai

261 In which year was Bhagat Singh executed by the British in India?

(a) 1931 (b) 1942 (c) 1858

262 Who in 1928 led the Civil Disobedience at Bardoli (sub-district of Surat) refusing to pay the enhanced land revenue?

(a) Mahatma Gandhi (b) Vallabhbhai Patel (c) Morarji Desai

263 Who was the leader of the Indian National
Army that aimed to remove by force British rule in India?

(a) Subhas Chandra Bose (b) Bhagat Singh
(c) Mohammed Ali Jinnah

264 Annie Besant was the first woman
president of the congress session held at Calcutta.
Who was the first Indian woman to become
the president of the congress?

(a) Vijayalakshmi Pandit (b) Saojini Naidu
(c) Indira Gandhi

265 The Revolt of Champaran in 1914 is an
important event in Indian history. It led to the Champaran
Satyagraha by Mahatma Gandhi. Where is Champaran?

(a) Bihar (b) Madhya Pradesh (c) Chhattisgarh

266 Who was called the Iron Man of India?

(a) Subhas Chandra Bose (b) Vallabhbhai Patel
(c) J.R.D.Tata

267 Quit India movement was the Indian
freedom movement asking the British to leave.
When did this start?

(a)1911 (b) 1942 (c) 1947

268 In March 1930, Mahatma Gandhi
marched to the seashore to break the unjust salt
law imposed by the British Govt. Which
town on the seashore?

(a) Madras (b) Vijayavada (c) Dandi

269 Lala Lajapat Rai, the great freedom fighter,
was known as Punjab Kesari. (Lion of Punjab).
But which great freedom fighter started
the newspaper called Kesari?

(a) Madan Mohan Malaviya (b) Lokamanya Tilak
(c) Gopal Krishna Gokhale

270 Khudai Khidmatgar (Servants of God)
was the movement against the British rule in India. This
non-violent opposition was founded by whom?

(a) Mohammed Ali Jinnah (b) Khan Abdul Gafar Khan
(c) Maulana Abul Kalam Azad

271 " *Gita Rahasya*"a commentary on the
Bhagavadgita was written by this freedom fighter
whilst serving the jail sentence of six years
in Mandalay, Burma (now Myanmar). Who is the author?

(a) Gopal Krishna Gokhale (b) Aurobindo Ghoshe
(c) Lokamanya Tilak

272 The Ganesh festival as a public celebration
was introduced as a national movement by which
of the following leaders?

(a) Mahatma Gandhi (b) Lokamanya Tilak
(c) Acharya Kripalani

273 Calcutta (now Kolkata) was the capital

of British controlled India. Which city was the administrative capital during summer months since 1864?

(a) Dehra Dun (b) Shimla (c) Darjeeling

274 Mahatma Gandhi was jailed by the British several times. What is the total length of time he spent in prison?

(a) 4 years (b) 5 years (c) 7 years

275 As part of the British Empire, India supported Britain in the First World War. (1914-1918) How many Indians were recruited in the war effort?

(a) 50,000 (b) 400,000 (c) one million

276 How many Indian soldiers in the Indian division of the British army died in the First World War?

(a) 5,000 (b) 25,000 (c) 75,000

277 During the British rule of India, the famine of 1943-44 in West Bengal killed how many people?

(a) 100,000 (b) half a million (c) two million

278 How many Indians were in the British Indian Army in the Second World War?

(a) 500,000 (b) 1.5 million (c) 2.5 million

279 Who was the Prime Minister of Britain when India became independent?

(a) Ramsay McDonald (b) Clement Attlee
(c) Harold Macmillan

280 Who was the monarch on throne in Britain when India became independent?

(a) George V (b) George VI (c) Queen Elizabeth II

281 It was Chaudhuri Rahmat Ali and his group in Cambridge in England who coined the name Pakistan for the separate Muslim majority country after independence of India from the British rule. What were the initials standing for?

(a) Peshawar - Ahmedabad- Karachi
(b) Punjab-Afghan-Kashmir-Sind
(c) Punjab And Kashmir

282 At the time of the independence of India in 1947, many princely states were independent of direct British rule. They voluntarily joined the newly formed states of India. How many such independent princely states and estates existed at the time?

(a) 56 (b) 156 (c) 560

283 Who was the first Governor General of independent India?

(a) Lord Mountbatten (b) C. Rajagopalachari
(c) Rajendra Prasad

284 Who was the first President of India?

(a) Rajendra Prasad (b) Vallabhbhai Patel

(c) S. Radhakrishnan

285 He was the first Indian to become the Governor
General of India. Who was he?
(a) C.Rajagopalachari (b) K.M.Cariappa
(c) Vallabhbhai Patel

286 Who was the first woman Governor of a state in India?

(a) Sarojini Naidu (b) Padmaja Naidu
(c) Vijayalakshmi Pandit

287 Jawaharlal Nehru was the first Prime Minister
of India. How many years was he Prime Minister?

(a) 9 years (b) 11 years (c) 17 years

288 Who was the first woman Cabinet Minister of India?

(a) Indira Gandhi (b) Rajkumari Amrit Kaur
(c) Sucheta Kripalani

289 Who was the first Vice-President of India?

(a) S.Radhakrishnan (b) C. Rajagopalachari
(c) Zakir Husain

290 Who was the last Governor General of India?

(a) Lord Mountbatten (b) Rajendra Prasad
(c) C Rajagopalachari

291 She was the first woman Chief Minister
of a state. Who was she?

(a) Sucheta Kripalani (b) Sarojini Naidu
(c) Vijayalakshmi Pandit

292 Who was a staunch follower of Mahatma
Gandhi and is well known for his movement of the
Bhoodaan Yajna? (Land donation)

(a)Lal Bahadur Shastri (b) Lala Lajapat Rai (c) Vinoba
Bhave

293 Jawaharlal Nehru was the first Prime Minister
of India. Who was the second Prime Minister of India?

(a) Indira Gandhi (b) Morarji Desai (c) Lal Bahadur Shastri

294 The national song of India is "Vande Mataram".
Who is the author of it?

(a) Bankimchandra Chatterjee
(b) Sharat Chandra Chatterjee (c) Rabindranath Tagore

295 Who was the first Chief of Army Staff
of independent India?

(a) General K. M. Cariappa
(b) General Manekshaw (c) General K.S. Timmayya

296 When British rule ended in India, the newly
formed Pakistan declared independence on 14thAugust
1947. Who was the first Governor General of
Pakistan?

(a) Mohammed Ali Jinnah (b) AyubKhan
(c) Khan Abdul Gafar Khan

297 This President of India was the first Spalding Professor of Eastern Religions at Oxford University, England. Name him.

(a) S. Radhakrishnan (b) Rajendra Prasad
(c) V.V. Giri

298 Who was the first Field Marshal of independent India?

(a) Gen Manekshaw (b) Gen K.S.Timmayya
(c) Gen K.M.Cariappa

299 When did India become a republic?

(a) 1947 (b) 1950 (c) 1956

300 The region formerly known as East Pakistan became independent Bangladesh aided by India in that struggle. In which year?

(a) 1948 (b) 1961 (c) 1971

301 "*Amar Shonar Bangla*" is the National Anthem of Bangladesh. Who is the poet of this anthem?

(a) Bankim Chandra Chatterjee
(b) Rabindranath Tagore (c) Sarojini Naidu

302 When was Goa liberated from Portuguese occupation?

(a) 1949 (b) 1956 (c) 1961

303 The honour of becoming the first woman President of the General Assembly of the UNO goes to this Indian. Who is she?

(a) Vijayalakshmi Pandit (b) Rajakumari Amrit Kaur
(c) Padmaja Naidu

304 Sir Harilal J. Kania became the first Indian
to hold this position in independent India.
What position was it?

(a) High Commissioner to Britain (b) Foreign Minister
(c) Chief Justice of India

305 He was the first Law Minister of independent
India and is known for his major role in drafting the
Indian Constitution. Who is he?

(a) Maulana Abul Kalam Azad (b) Vallabhbhai Patel
(c) B.R.Ambedkar

306 Who is the head of the Republic of India?

(a) The Prime Minister (b) The President of India
(c) Chief Justice of the Supreme Court

307 In 1950 India became a republic. However,
the royal families of the erstwhile princely states of pre-
independent India were given payments called
the Privy Purse. This privilege was abolished by the
Govt of India as in a republic every citizen is
equal.When was it?

(a) 1956 (b) 1971 (c) 1984

308 Gandhi jayanti is on October 2nd.Which of
the following Indian Prime Ministers was also born
on 2nd October?

(a) Indira Gandhi (b) Lal Bahadur Shastri (c) Morarji Desai

309 Teachers' Day is celebrated on 5th September,
in honour of which of the following?

(a) Zakir Husain (b) V.V.Giri (c) S. Radhakrishnan

310 Who is called the Nightingale of India?

(a) Sarojini Naidu (b) M.S. Subbulakshmi
(c) Lata Mangeshkar

311 Who gave a call to the nation for a "Total Revolution"?

(a) Jayaprakash Narayan (b) Morarji Desai
(c) Babasaheb Ambedkar

312 "Jai Jawan, Jai Kisan " was the call
by which Prime Minister?

(a) Indira Gandhi (b) Lal Bahadur Shastri (c) Charan Singh

313 The Twenty-Point Programme was
launched to eradicate poverty and to improve the
quality of life. Which Prime Minister
launched that programme?

(a) Morarji Desai (b) Charan Singh (c) Indira Gandhi

314 After the independence of India, the invasion
of China seeking the Indian territory led to Sino-Indian war.
When was it?

(a) 1949 (b) 1956 (c) 1962

315 How long did the Sino-Indian war last?

(a) one month (b) six months (c) one year

316 Aksai Chin is the area China occupied following the Sino-India war. Aksai Chin was earlier a part of which of the following?

(a) Sikkim (b) Arunachal Pradesh (c) Kashmir

317 Since the Independence and partition of India in 1947 into India and Pakistan, how many wars have taken place between Pakistan and India?

(a) Two (b) Four (c) Seven

318 Tashkent Declaration is a Peace agreement between

(a) India and China (b) India and Pakistan
(c) India and Russia

319 What is the minimum age limit to be eligible to become a Member of the Lok Sabha (MP – Member of Parliament)?

(a) 25 years (b) 30 years (c) 35 years

320 What is the minimum age limit to be eligible to become a member of the Rajya Sabha?

(a) 25 years (b) 30 years (c) 35 years

321 What is the minimum age limit to be eligible to become the President of India?

(a) 30 years (b) 35 years (c) 40 years

322 What is the minimum age limit to be eligible
to become the Prime Minister of India?

(a) 25 years (b) 45 years (c) 50 years

323 The Commonwealth of Nations is an
inter-governmental organization. The member states
are erstwhile colonies of the British empire.
India is a member. How many members
are in this organization?

(a) 102 (b) 73 (c) 54

324 Where is the headquarters of the
Commonwealth of Nations?

(a) Colombo (b) Karachi (c) London

325 All independent countries exchange
ambassadors with other countries for international
communication. Commonwealth countries
exchange High Commissioners (not ambassadors).
Who was the first Indian High Commissioner
to Britain?

(a) Morarji Desai (b) T.N. Kaul (c) Vijayalakshmi Pandit

326 The German ship Emden shelled this
Indian city in 1914. This was the only Indian city attacked
in the first World War by Germans.
Which city was it?

(a) Madras (Chennai) (b) Bombay (Mumbai)

(c) Thiruvananthpuram

327 This city is called City of Prime ministers. Which city is it?

(a) New Delhi (b) Allahabad (c) Lucknow

328 Who founded the Sikh Holy City Amritsar?

(a) Guru Ramdas (b) Guru Gobindsingh (c) Guru Nanak

329 The old city Delhi was known as Dhillika. When was it established?

(a)CE 736 (b) CE 1193 (c) CE 1026

330 Previously this city was known as Prayag. By what name is it known now?

(a) Ajmer (b) Allahabad (c) Ahmedabad

331Meaning of the name of which of the following cities is thought to be "city of virtue"?

(a) Kanchipuram (b) Pune (c) Varanasi (Benares)

332 Ayuthia the ancient capital of Thailand was named after which Indian city?

(a) Ayodhya (b) Alakapuri (c) Amaravati

333 Sir Edwin Lutyens and Sir Herbert Baker planned this city. Name it.

(a) New Delhi (b) Dehra Dun (c) Darjeeling

334 The French architect Le Carbusier planned this city. Which city?

(a) Chandigarh (b) Bengaluru (c) Pondicherry

335 When was the city of New Delhi completed and officially inaugurated?

(a) 1931 (b) 1942 (c) 1947

336 In 1935 Reserve Bank of India was established by the British. It is India's Central Bank and was based in Calcutta (Kolkata). Its headquarters are now situated in

(a) Bengaluru (b) New Delhi (c) Mumbai

337 Job Charnock of the East India Company founded this town in CE 1686 - 90 as a trading port. Which one?

a)Madras(Chennai) (b) Calcutta(Kolkata) (c) Mumbai (Bombay)

338 When did the Indian state of the Punjab divide into the Punjab and Haryana?

(a) 1956 (b) 1966 (c) 1971

339 The Sun temple of Konark is a UNESCO World Heritage Site. Where is this famous temple of architectural excellence?

(a) Odisha (b) Madhya Pradesh (c) Andhra Pradesh

340 The famous Dilwara temples of
Jain religion are situated in

(a) Rajasthan (b) Bihar (c) Andhra Pradesh

341 Where can you see the Vivekananda Memorial Rock?

(a) Kolkata (b) Kanyakumari (c) Bengaluru

342 Kailasanath temple is a famous rock-
cut temple of architectural excellence. Where is it?

(a) Varanasi (b) Ellora (c) Kanchi

343 Where is the largest Temple complex for a Hindu God?

(a) Angkor Wat in Cambodia
(b) Anuradhapura in Sri Lanka
(c) Kandahar in Afghanistan

344 Hawa Mahal (the Palace of Winds) is situated in:

(a) Jaipur (b) Agra (c) Fatepur Sikri

345 Swami Vivekananda International airport
serves which city?

(a) Kolkata (b) Raipur (c) Bengaluru

346 Salar Jung museum is a famous museum.
Where is it situated?

(a) Shrinagar (b) Jaipur (c) Hyderabad

347 Raj Ghat in New Delhi is a memorial

to which of the following?
(a) Indira Gandhi (b) Mahatma Gandhi (c) Rajiv Gandhi

348 If you land in Chatrapati Shivaji
International Airport, where would you be?

(a)Bhopal (b) Indore (c) Mumbai

349 The lion capital of the Ashoka Pillar
is adopted as the emblem of the Republic of India. The
pillar was erected by Emperor Ashoka in the
third century BCE. Where was this pillar found?

(a) Sarnath (b) Lumbini (c) Kapilavastu

350 Emperor Ashoka converted to Buddhism.
He built *stupas*. Scattered all over his kingdom, how many
such *stupas* is he reputed to have built?

(a) 84 (b) 840 (c) 84,000

351 The Kailasanath temple at Ellora is a
magnificent work of architecture. Who built it?

(a) Pallava kings (b) Rashtrakuta kings (c) Pandya kings

352 Built in the 16th century, the Charminar
is a famous Islamic architecture. Where is
it?

(a) Ahmedabad (b) Ajmer (c) Hyderabad

353 Ashtadhyayi is the famous work of Sanskrit
grammar compiled in fifth century BCE. Who is its author?

(a) Panini (b) Patanjali (c) Yajnavalkya

354 Charaka is a famous ancient Indian. What was he?

(a) Astronomer (b) Physician (c) Mathematician

355 Who was the famous ancient Indian surgeon?

(a) Yajnavalkya (b) Sushruta (c) Charvaka

356 Which is the only state in independent
India giving Sanskrit the status of an official
language of the state?

(a) Kerala (b) Kashmir (c) Uttarakhand

357 Arthashastra is a famous ancient book
on statecraft. Who is its author?

(a) Manu (b) Kautilya (c) Patanjali

358 Which poet of Sanskrit is called the *Adi Kavi*
(the first poet)?

(a) Valmiki (b) Vyasa (c) Kalidasa

359 Which was the first ever Sanskrit
work published in English translation?

(a) The Bhagavadgita (b) Meghadoota (c) The Ramayana

360 The epic the Mahabharata is the world's
longest poem. Who was its author?

(a) Kalidasa (b) Vyasamaharshi (c) Bhavabhuti

361 Complete canon of Buddhist scriptures
was first written in which language?

(a) Nepalese (b) Sanskrit (c) Pali

362 The Urdu language developed in India.
What is the meaning of the word Urdu?

(a) Muslim (b) Camp (c) Ghazal

363 " Discovery of India" is a famous book.
Who is its author?

(a) Vasco da Gama (b) R.K.Narayan (c) Jawaharlal Nehru

364 Tughlaq-i-Hind is a famous book.
Who is its author?

(a) Alberuni (b) Ibn Battuta (c) Mohammad bin Tughlaq

365 Which was the first language recognized
by Govt of India as a classical language?

(a) Hindi (b) Tamil (c) Sanskrit

366 Who is the author of the epic the Ramayana

(a) Bhasa (b) Valmiki (c) Panini

367 Who was the person that first deciphered
in CE 1837 the ancient Brahmi script?

(a) James Prinsep (b) Sir William Jones (c) Max Muller

368 In which language did Mahavira,

the founder of Jain religion, preach?
(a) Ardhamagadhi (b) Sanskrit (c) Prakrit

369 Telugu, Tamil and Malayalam are Dravidian
languages. Which of the following
languages is another major Dravidian language?

(a)Marathi (b) Oriya (c) Kannada

370 *Abhijnanashakuntalam* is the first ever
Sanskrit play published in English translation. It
was published in 1789.Who wrote the
original Sanskrit play?

(a) Kalidasa (b) Bhavabhuti (c) Bhasa

371 What script is used to write Hindi?

(a) Brahmi (b) Kharoshti (c) Devanagari

372 Vishnusharma is the author of the famous book.
Which one of the following?

(a) Kumarasambhava (b) Panchatantra (c) Kadambari

373 The Government of India has recognized
both Kannada and Telugu as classical languages.
Which of the following was recognized as a
classical language after Tamil was recognized as a
classical language?

(a) Hindi (b) Sanskrit (c) Bengali

374 The 12th-century work *Rajatarangini*
by Kalhana describes the royal lineage of

which kingdom in India?
(a) Kerala (b) Kashmir (c) Gujarat

375 *Shangam* literature is associated with which language?

(a) Oriya (b) Tamil (c) Assamese

376 This ancient king is known for his literary works
Ratnavali and *Priyadarshika*. Who is this king?

(a) Harsha (b) Vikramaditya (c) Chandragupta

377 One of the most famous ancient literary
works is *Shilappadigaram*. (Tale of the Anklet)In which
language is it written?

(a) Tamil (b) Kannada (c) Oriya

378 *Mudrarakshasa* (signet ring of Rakshasa)
is a famous Sanskrit play. Name its author.

(a) Kalidasa (b) Vishakhadatta (c) Bharavi

379 *Tolkappiyam* is one of the earliest works
of literature in India. In which language?

(a) Sanskrit (b) Tamil (c) Malayalam

380 *Ramacharitamanas* is a great literary work
in Hindi. Who is its author?

(a) Chaitanya (b) Tulasidas (c) Kabirdas

381 Which state in India has the highest literacy rate?

(a) Meghalaya (b) Kerala (c) Bihar

382 This poet saint was a weaver by occupation and lived in Varanasi. (CE 1440 - 1518). Who was it?

(a) Guru Nanak (b) Tukaram (c) Kabirdas

383 These caves discovered in 1973 in India have the largest collection of pre-historic paintings said to be 6,000 years old. Where are these caves?

(a) Ajanta caves (b) Bhimbetka caves (c) Elephanta caves

384 The Ajanta caves, the pride of Indian ancient art, have preserved the most beautiful paintings of our ancestors. Where are the Ajanta caves?

(a) Odisha (b) Rajasthan (c) Maharashtra

385 Kanchi in Tamil Nadu is one of the seven holy cities for Hindu pilgrimage. What is the famous temple in Kanchi?

(a) Sarasvati (b) Lakshmi (c) Kamakshi

386 Where in India is the tallest monolithic statue?

(a) Karnataka (b) Kashmir (c) Bihar

387 Whose statue is the tallest monolithic statue in India?

(a) Lord Shiva (b) The Buddha (c) Bahubali

388 Qutub Minar in Delhi was built in the 13th century. How tall is it?

(a) 109 feet (b) 177 feet (c) 238 feet.

389 The monolithic statue of Bahubali (Gommateshvara) is in Shravana Belgola (Karnataka). How tall is this tallest monolithic statue?

(a) 77 feet (b) 57 feet (c) 49 feet

390 The famous stupa at Sanchi in Madhya Pradesh is one of the extant stupas in India. What is a stupa?

(a) Burial mounds of relics of the Buddhist saints
(b) Places where the Buddha preached
(c) Places where the Buddhist saints meditated

391 This city is famous for the 16th-17th century Meenakshi temple. Which city?

(a) Mathura in Uttar Pradesh
(b) Matheran in Maharashtra
(c) Madura in Tamil Nadu

392 The Elephanta caves are on an island west of Mumbai. How did the name Elephanta come to that island?

(a) Wild elephants on the island
(b) Finding of a huge rock elephant statue on the island
(c) Place for taming elephants

393 The Gateway of India was built to commemorate the visit of King George V of Britain. It was inaugurated in 1934. Where is this impressive structure?

(a) New Delhi (b) Mumbai (c) Kolkata

394 India Gate is a magnificent structure.
Where can you see it?

(a) Chennai (b) Bengaluru (c) New Delhi

395 Bharata Ratna is the highest civilian
honour that was introduced in 1954. Which of
the following was its first ever recipient ?

(a) C.V. Raman (b) Jawaharlal Nehru (c) Rajendra Prasad

396 Srinivasa Ramanujan is considered a
genius for his great original works. In which
field is he famous?

(a) Chemistry (b) Mathematics (c) Physics

397 Khudadad Khan was the first Indian
to receive this medal. Which medal?

(a) Olympic Gold Medal (b) Victoria Cross Medal
(c) Humanitarian Medal

398 Jnanapitha award is an annual literary
national award instituted in 1961. Who was the
first recipient of this prestigious award?

(a) G. Shankar Kurup (b) Umashankar Joshi
(c) D.R. Bendre

399 Who was the first Indian to win the Nobel Prize?

(a) Rabindranath Tagore (b) C.V. Raman

(c) Harobind Khorana

400 The Booker Prize for literature is a prestigious
award given in the United Kingdom. Who was
the first Indian to receive this prize?

(a)R.K. Narayan (b) Arundhati Roy (c) Aravind Adiga

401 This Indian renounced a knighthood
in protest of Jalianwala bagh massacre in
1919. Who was it?

(a) Rabindranath Tagore (b) C.P.Ramaswamy Iyer
(c) C V Raman

402 Who was given in 1877 the title of Kaiser-i-Hind?

(a) Queen Victoria (b) Bahadur Shah II (c) Nadir Shah

403 Ramon Magsaysay award is a prestigious
award in Asia named after the past President of the
Philippines and is given annually. It started
in 1958. Who was the first Indian to have the honour of
receiving this award in 1958?

(a) Jawaharlal Nehru (b) S.Radhakrishnan
(c) Vinoba Bhave

404 Dadasaheb Phalke award is a prestigious
national award in film industry. Who was its first-
ever recipient in 1969?

(a) M.G. Ramachandran (b) Satyajit Ray (c) Devika Rani

405 This English poet won the Nobel Prize

for literature. He was born in Bombay
(Mumbai). Who was the poet?

(a) W.B. Yeats (b) Rudyard Kipling (c) T.S.Eliot

406 This famous Indian singer received
the Magsaysay award. Who was it?

(a) Lata Mangeshkar (b) M.S. Subbulakshmi
(c) Bhimsen Joshi

407 The Hindus were the first to use the symbol
zero and the decimal system in mathematics. Where on the
stone-wall of a temple can we find the earliest
record of zero mentioned?

(a) Ujjayini (b) Thiruvananatapuram (c) Gwalior

408 Who was this ancient Indian astronomer
and mathematician who said that the earth is a globe
and is rotating on its own axis?

(a) Brahmagupta (b) Parameshvar (c) Aryabhata

409 Maharaja Jai Singh built the famous
architectural astronomical observatory in the 18th century.
Where is it?

(a) Jaipur (b) Agra (c) Ujjayini

410 Who was the first Indian scientist to get a Nobel Prize?

(a)C.V.Raman (b) Hargobind Khorana
(c) C. Subrahmanyan

411 In the atomic structure types of subatomic particles are named in honour of the scientists who discovered the properties of such particles.
Which type of particles is named after an Indian scientist?

(a) Lepton (b) Boson (c) Gluon

412 An ancient school of Indian philosophy founded by Kanada proposed that all physical objects are made up of small particles called *'paramanu'*. These ideas echo in the distant past the scientific discoveries of modern man. What is the name of this ancient philosophical school?

(a) Sankhya school (b) Mimamsa (c) Vaisheshika

413 The element Helium was for the first time discovered by experiments conducted in India. Where in India were these observational experiments conducted?

(a) Guntur in Andhra Pradesh (b) Jaipur in Rajasthan (c) Varanasi in Uttar Pradesh

414 When was the first nuclear test of India carried out?

(a) 1957 (b) 1967 (c) 1974

415 Raman Research Institute was established by the Nobel Prize winning physicist Sir C. V. Raman. Where is it?

(a) Chennai (b) Hyderabad (c) Bengaluru

416 Who is considered the father of Indian Space

Research Programme?

(a) C.V.Raman (b) Vikram Sarabhai (c) Homi J. Bhabha

417 Name the Indian scientist, who, along
with Albert Einstein, formulated a law of
quantum mechanics

(a) Satyen Bose (b) Sir C. V.Raman
(c) Chandrasekhar Subrahmanyan

418 This famous British scientist emigrated
to India in 1957 and took Indian citizenship.Who is he?

(a) J. B. S. Haldane (b) Ronald Ross (c) Alexander Fleming

419 Who is the Indian scientist famous for his
pioneering research in electromagnetic waves and
plant physiology?

(a) Prafulla Chandra Ray (b) Jagadish Chandra Bose
(c) Meghanad Saha

420 Lilavati is a famous book on mathematics
written by the 12th century illustrious
mathematician Bhaskaracharya. The mathematical
problems in this book are addressed to Lilavati,
who appears to be very intelligent and very
interested in mathematics. What relation was Lilavati to the
author Bhskaracharya?

(a)Wife (b) Daughter (c) Sister

421Brahmagupta lived in the 7th century CE.
What is he famous as?

(a) Architect (b) Mathematician (c) Astrologer

422 This Nobel Prize-winning English doctor
discovered the parasite responsible for the
dreaded disease Malaria. He discovered it in Calcutta (now
Kolkata). He was born in India. Who is he?

(a)William Leishman (b) Ronald Ross (c) Charles Donovan

423 Sir William Jones is credited for establishing
in 1784 in British India. What was it?

(a) Police Force of Calcutta (b) Asiatic Society
(c) Hospital for the poor

424 An explosive charge is named after an
Indian city where it was invented in 1912. The explosive
device was used by the combat engineers in the First World
War and is used even today in war zones all over the
world.What is it called?

(a) Calcutta Torpedo (b) Bangalore Torpedo
(c) Madras Torpedo

425 Where was India's first nuclear test carried out?

(a) Rajasthan (b) Odisha (c) Kerala

426 The Govt of India established in 1962
the Equatorial Rocket Launching Station at Thumba.
Where is Thumba?

(a) Kerala (b) Andhra Pradesh (c) Tamil Nadu

427 India has successfully launched space satellites.

What name was given to the first Indian satellite?

(a) Aryabhata (b) Rohini (c) Agni

428 The first Indian satellite was launched into orbit in 1975. Where was it launched?

(a) Thumba (b) Soviet Union Cosmodrome (c) Kennedy Space Centre, USA

429 The Indian Space Research Organization (ISRO) was established in 1969. Where is the head office ofISRO?

(a) New Delhi (b) Chennai (c) Bengaluru

430 Who was the first Indian to travel in space?

(a) Rakesh Sharma (b) Kalpana Chawla (c) Ravish Malhotra

431 The National Aerospace Laboratory is India's advanced research centre. Where is it?

(a) Hyderabad (b) Bengaluru (c) New Delhi

432 The Satish Dhawan Space Centre is situated at

(a) Sriharikota (b) Mumbai (c) Kolkata

433 The Bhabha Atomic Research Centre (BARC) is the nuclear research centre established in 1954. Where is it situated?
(a) Bengaluru (b) Thiruvananthapuram (c) Mumbai

434 Chandrayaan - 1 was the satellite
launched in October 2008 and successfully orbited
the Moon. Where was it launched?

(a) Sriharikota (b) Thumba (c) Bengaluru

435 The successful deliberate crash landing
of the Moon Impact Probe (MIP) by the Chandrayaan -1
satellite placed the tricolor Indian flag on
the Moon. How many countries placed their flags
on the Moon before India ?

(a) 3 (b) 5 (c) 7

436 J.R.D.Tata is known as an industrialist and
philanthropist. He was the first person to
start in India which of the following?

(a) Commercial Airlines (b) Shipping industry
(c) Electricity supply company

437 India has one of the largest railway networks
in the world.What is the total approximate length of the
route covered by this network ?

(a) 10,000 km (b) 39,000 km (c) 65,000 km

438 Amrita Sher Gil, Vyasa, Kalidasa, Valmiki,
Tyagaraja are Indian names for craters on a planet in the
solar system. On which planet are these craters
honouring the Indian artistes and writers and poets?

(a) Mercury (b) Jupiter (c) Neptune
439 Lakshmi Planum is the mountain plateau

on which planet? It is named after the Indian goddess
Lakshmi.
(a) Mars (b) Venus (c) Saturn

440 The first Indian feature film was

(a) Raja Harishchandra (b) Parvatiparinaya
(c) Bharatamata

441 The first talking Indian film was released in 1931.
Which one?

(a) Alam Ara (b) Mandodari - Sita (c) Taramati

442 This city boasts of the largest integrated
film city in the world. Which city?

(a) Bengaluru (b) Hyderabad (c) Mumbai

443 The famous institution J.J. School of Arts
was founded in the 1860s. Where is it?

(a) Kolkata (b) New Delhi (c) Mumbai

444 The nineteenth century painter
Raja Ravi Varma is famous for his paintings of the
Ramayana and Mahabharata. Where is he from?

(a) Rajasthan (b) West Bengal (c) Kerala

445 Amrita Sher Gil was a famous 20th-century
Indian artist who died at the age of 28. Who was she?

(a) Actress (b) Painter (c) Musician
446 *Natyashastra* (the study of Dramatic Arts)

is a famous book of ancient times. Who is its author?
(a) Bharatamuni (b) Kautilya (c) Patanjali

447 Kathakali is a classical dance.
Where did it originate?

(a) Tamil Nadu (b) Karnataka (c) Kerala

448 Kuchipudi is a classical dance and is
centuries old. It is said its name is from the town where
this dance form originated. Where is it from?

(a) Andhra Pradesh (b) Karnataka (c) Odisha

449 The Indian classical music has two main
systems. Hindustani is most popular in north India. What is
the second one that happens to be more
popular in south India?

(a) Carnatic music (b) Tamil music (c) Southern music

450 Mridangam is a very important and essential
musical instrument used in Carnatic music. What kind of
instrument is it?

(a) Stringed instrument (b) Percussion instrument
(c) Wind instrument

451 Khasi and Garo are associated with Meghalaya.
What are they?

(a) Languages (b) Mountains (c) Dances

452 Which of the following states has Christian
religion as a majority religion?

(a) Kerala (b) Arunachal Pradesh (c) Nagaland

453 Who exclaimed that " East is East and West
is West. The twain shall never meet".

(a) Swami Vivekananda
(b) Mahatma Gandhi (c) Rudyard Kipling

454 What was the name given to the Indian
division in the British army in the Second World War
fighting in Burma? (1939-45)

(a) Sepoy Army (b) Chindits (c) Coolie Army

455 What is the name of the village that
has given a name to an infantry bullet?

(a) Dum Dum (b) Palam (c) Deolali

456 What was the literacy rate
in India before independence?

(a) 15% (b) 35 % (c) 47%

457 Anandi Joshi(1865 -1887) was the first
Indian woman to do what ?

(a) Qualify as a Doctor of Medicine (b) Qualify as lawyer
(c) First female novelist

458 Who designed the tricolor National Flag of India?

(a) Pingali Venkayya (b) Raja Ravi Varma
(c) C.Rajagopalachari

459 The blue wheel known as the Dharma
Chakra at the centre of the Indian National flag is taken
from the Dharma Chakra of Ashoka the Buddhist
emperor of ancient India. How many
spokes are in this wheel?

(a) 22 (b) 23 (c) 24

460 Cornelia Sorabji is the first Indian
woman to become what?

(a) Barrister (b) Airline Pilot (c) Professor of Sanskrit

461 Several words in English language are
derived from many Indian languages.Out of the list of the
words here -sugar, cash, opal, virus, beryl,
bandicoot, shampoo, jaggery, juggernaut- which words
are from an Indian language?

(a) Sugar and opal (b) Cash and juggernaut
(c) All the words in this list

462 How many languages are recognized
as the national languages of India?

(a)7 (b) 13 (c) 20

463 A style of breeches worn by horse riders
is named after this Indian city. Which city?

(a) Hyderabad (b) Jodhpur (c) Lucknow

464 The first ever introduction of using human
fingerprints to detect criminals was by the British

in India. When was it?

(a) 1858 (b) 1901 (c) 1930

465 Which state in India has the highest number of domesticated elephants?

(a) Rajasthan (b) Odisha (c) Kerala

466 Jaganmohan Palace is a famous palace and art gallery. Where is it situated?

(a) Dwaraka (b) Jagannathpuri (c) Mysore

467 Which city is famous for its shipping industry?

(a) Vishakhapattanam (b) Chennai (c) Mangaluru

468 What is a Bombay duck?

(a) Goose (b) Swan (c) Fish

469 Camellia species of plant is grown in India for centuries. India is famous for a few special varieties of it. India is a major exporter of it. What is this plant?

(a) Rice (b) Cotton (c) Tea

470 The national census is conducted every ten years. When was the first census held in India?

(a) 1881 (b) 1901 (c) 1951

471 What is the National bird of India?

(a) Crow (b) Parrot (c) Peacock

472 What is the national flower of India?

(a) Lotus (b) Jasmine (c) Parijata

473 Calico is a type of rough cloth that
was developed in India. Its name comes from

(a) Calcutta (b) Calicut (c) Cochin

474 Which is the first Indian city to have
underground trains for public transport?

(a) New Delhi (b) Bengaluru (c) Kolkata

475 What is the national animal of India?

(a) Cow (b) Tiger (c) Elephant

476 What is the national tree of India?

(a)Pipal (b) Banyan (c) Mango

477 Sandalwood is a fragrant wood
with commercial importance. Its wood is sacred to
Hindus and its oil is used as scent.
Where in India is it grown mostly?

(a) Karnataka (b) Kashmir (c) Meghalaya

478 Kohinoor is the famous diamond
from India, now displayed in the Tower of London,
in England. What is the meaning

of the word Koh – i -- noor?

(a) Mountain of Light (b) Queen of diamonds
(c) King of diamonds

479 Where in India was the first passenger
train service started in 1853? Between –

(a) Bombay and Thane (b) Calcutta and Delhi
(c) Hyderabad and Madras

480 Which is the only city in India where a
tram service is provided as a form of public transport?

(a) Jaipur (b) Bengaluru (c) Kolkata

481 Jim Corbett National Park is a wildlife
sanctuary named after the British hunter of tigers and
conservationist James Corbett. Where is it?

(a) West Bengal (b) Uttarakhand (c) Assam

482 NH 44 is the National Highway passes through a few
states. Which following cities does it connect?

(a) Kanyakumari to Kolkata (b) Kanyakumari to Mumbai
(c) Kanyakumari to Varanasi

483 Zuben Mehta is the first Indian to become the
Conductor of what?

(a) New York Philharmonic Orchestra
(b) London Philharmonic Orchestra
(c) Chicago Philharmonic Orchestra
484 In which city in India one can see human-

pulled rikshaw as a mode of public transport?

(a) Gandhinagar (b) Chandigarh (c) Kolkata

485 The English channel is a 22 mile sea between
the south coast of England and the north coast of France.
Many men and women have swum this channel.
Who was the first Indian swimmer to achieve this feat?

(a)Mihir Sen (b) Arati Saha (c) Dolly Nazir

486 Calcutta Cricket Club is the first known
cricket club in India. When was it established?

(a) 1792 (b) 1901 (c) 1923

487 Kalaripayattu is an Indian martial arts that
has been practised for several centuries.
Where did it originate?

(a) Punjab (b) Kerala (c) Mizoram

488 Which sport was invented in India by the British?

(a) Cricket (b) Rugby (c) Snooker

489 Who was the first cricket test captain of India?

(a) C.K. Nayadu (b) Syed Mushtaq Ali
(c) Ghanashyamasimhji

490 The Indian game "kabaddi" gets its name
from which language?

(a) Tamil (b) Hindi (c) Punjabi

491 This card game originated in India. Which one?
(a) Cribbage (b) Auction Bridge (c) Poker

492 Yubi Lakpi is a field game with seven team members passing a coconut as a ball. Where is it most popular?

(a) Mizoram (b) Manipur (c) Meghalaya

493 Which of the following games originated in India?

(a) Chess (b) Backgammon (c) Black Jack

494 Several English expressions or names are related to or associated with our country. Examples are Indonesia, India rubber, India ink etc.
Which of the following is named after India?

(a) Chemical element Indium (b) Indian Ocean
(c) Indian summer

495 Here is a quotation: "We owe a lot to the Indians, who taught us how to count, without which no worthwhile scientific discovery could have been made." This is a great but deserving appreciation of the mathematical achievement of our ancestors. Who said this?

(a)Albert Einstein (b) Bill Gates (c) Arthur Eddington

496 India is a member of the organization called the G20. What does the letter G stand for?

(a) Great Achievers (b) Group (c) Grand Economies
497 A chemical leak from the Union Carbide

chemicals industry on 2nd December 1984 killed
about 4000 people in their sleep and injured
half a million people. In which city did this horrendous
tragedy happen?

(a)Nagpur (b) Indore (c) Bhopal

498 Which is the busiest airport in India in terms of number
of passengers?

(a) New Delhi (b) Kolkata (c) Bengaluru

499 *Satyamevajayate* (Truth alone prevails)
is the national motto of the Republic of India and
accompanies the National Emblem – the
four-lion capital. From where does this sacred
Sanskrit saying come?

(a) The Rig Veda (b) Mundaka Upanishad (c) Bhagavadgita

500 Who lives at 7 Race Course Road, New Delhi?

(a) The Chief Justice of India
(b) The Chief of Army of India
(c) The Prime Minister of India

501 In a BBC (United Kingdom) survey of
public voting, Mahatma Gandhi was declared "Man of the
Millennium". In a few other such public surveys
he was voted the Man of The Millennium.Here is
a famous quotation about Mahatma Gandhi following his
assassination on 30th January 1948 in New Delhi.
"Generations to come will scarce believe that
such a one as this ever in flesh and blood walked

upon this earth." Who said it?

(a) Jawaharlal Nehru (b) George Bernard Shaw
(c) Albert Einstein

ANSWERS & EXPLANATIONS

1 (a) Six countries.

Russia, Canada, China, United States of America, Brazil and Australia – in descending order of area - are larger than India.

2 (b) 29 states

3 (a) Seven.

(Chandigarh, New Delhi, Daman and Diu, Dadra and Nagar Haveli, Lakshadweep islands, Puducherry, Andaman and Nicobar islands.)

4 (a) Goa

5 (b) Ganga

(Ganga is about 2600 km. The longest river in the world is the Nile in the Sudan and Egypt. It is 6695 km, which is about two and a half times as long as the Ganga. Thirty rivers in the world are longer than Ganga. The Sindhu River flows mostly in Pakistan and it is 3180 km.)

6 (c) Rajasthan

7 (a) Narmada

8 (a) 8 degrees north of equator

(It is 8.08^0 north latitude.)

9 (a) Sikkim

10 (b) 82.5^0 East

11 (b) Mirzapur (Uttar Pradesh)

12 (c) Mumbai

13 (a) Manas Sarovar

14 (a) Yarlung-Tsangpo

15 (b) Rajasthan

16 (b) 2900 km

17 (a) Kaveri river in Karnataka

18 (c) Tehri dam across Bhagirathi river in Uttarakhand. It is 855 feet (260 m) high.

19 (b) Mizoram

20 (a) Goa

21 (b) Goa

22 (b) Nine

(Gujarat, Maharashtra, Goa, Karnataka, Kerala, Tamil

Nadu, Andhra Pradesh, Odisha and West Bengal)

23 (a) 2900 km (almost the same length
as the Brahmaputra river.)

24 (b) Gujarat

25 (c) 3210 km

(North to south is about 300 km
longer than west to east borders of India.)

26 (a) Rajasthan

27 (a) 16,000 km

28 (b) Western-most place

29 (a) Declared and agreed in August 1947
the border line between India and Pakistan

30 (a) India and China boundary line.

31 (c) Meghalaya

(Cherrapunjee is a variant spelling. Rainfall can be more
than 400 inches a year!)

32 (c) Sikkim

33 (a) 1,750 km

34 (a) 2,500 km

(It is almost the same as the length of the river Ganga)

35 (a) 1,600 km

36 (c) Arunachal Pradesh

37 (b) Arunachal Pradesh

38 (a) Kanchenjunga (also spelt Kangchenjunga)

(Kanchenjunga is 28,169 feet and is the third highest in the world after Mt Everest 29,029 feet in Nepal and K2 in China-Pakistan region is 28,251 feet. Kanchenjunga is at the border of India and Nepal. Also the accuracy measurement of the height is affected by the snow accumulated at the mountain top! Mt Everest is now said to be 29,035 feet high.)

39 (a) Silvassa

40 (c) Between Tamil Nadu and Sri Lanka

41(a) Bhagirathi.

42 (b) Damodar river

43 (b) West Bengal

44 (a) Five states.

(Uttarakhand, Uttar Pradesh, Bihar, Jharkhand and West Bengal.)

45 (c) Nohkalikai in Meghalaya. It is 1,100 feet tall.

(Many waterfalls are not single-tier falls. Measurement varies and description varies in such situations. For comparison, the tallest single fall in the world is Angel Falls in Venezuela, South America. It is 3,212 feet tall. Angel Falls was named after the American aviator Jimmie Angel who discovered it first.)

46 (c) @ 600 km (see the map)

47 (c) Seven-Sister states

48 (a) Godavari (1,465 km.)

49 (b) Sutlaj (also spelt Sutlej)

50 (a) Saraswati river

51 (a) Karnataka

52 (a) Kashmir

(World's second highest peak, K2, is in this range but it is not in India.)

53 (a) Pakistan-Afghanistan

54 (c) Uttar Pradesh.
It has common border with eight states.

55 (b) Five Treasure Houses of Great Snow

56 (a) Hooghly (Hoogli)

57 (a) Hooghly

58 (b) Seven

(Pakistan, Afghanistan, China, Nepal, Bhutan, Myanmar and Bangladesh). For comparison, both China and Russia have common borders with 14 countries each. Brazil has common borders with ten countries!

59 (a) 17 states

60 (b) Eight states

(From west to east it passes through Gujarat, Rajasthan, Madhya Pradesh, Chhattisgarh, Jharkhand, West Bengal, Tripura and Mizoram.)

61 (a) Five states

(Uttar Pradesh, Madhya Pradesh, Chhattisgarh, Odisha and Andhra Pradesh.)

62 (c) Jhelum

63 (b) Assam

64 (c) New Town

65 (c) 570 islands

(This archipelago has approximately 570 islands.)

66 (a) Mahi river

67 (b) Karnataka

(Kolar gold fields and Hatti in Raichur district are famous. Gold is mined also in Jharkhand and Andhra Pradesh.)

68 (a) Andhra Pradesh

69 (c) Ujjayini

70 (a) Pakistan

71 (c) Brahmaputra

(Continuation in Bangladesh is called the Padma River before entering the Bay of Bengal.)

72 (c) Aizawl

73(b) Wular lake in Kashmir.

Kolleru lake in Andhra Pradesh is the second largest by area. (Sambhar lake in Rajasthan is the largest salt-water lake in India.)

74 (a) Lakshadweep

75 (a) Kashyapa rishi.

(The word mir is from Sanskrit meaning a lake. Kashyap's lake became Kashmir, according to a theory.)

76 (b) Kanyakumari
(At the latitude of 8.08^0 north and 77.5^0 East longitude.)

77 (a) Between Andaman and Nicobar islands.

(The channel is at 10^0 north latitude, that is how it got its name.)

78 (b) Ganga

79 (a) Andaman island

80 (a) Southern-most tip of Nicobar island.

(It is at 6^0 north latitude. However, the mainland's southern-most tip, Kanyakumari, is at 8^0 north latitude. See question No.76.)

81 (a) Near Manas Sarovar

82 (b) Mahanadi in Odisha

83 (a) Andhra Pradesh

84 (b) Kaveri

85 (c) Sikkim

86 (b) Kerala

87 (a) Avatar Singh Cheema.

He climbed it in May 1965. (In 1984, Bachendri Pal became the first Indian woman to climb Mt Everest. However, Tenzing Norgay, the first man ever to climb Mt. Everest, on 29 May 1953, was a Nepalese citizen. He was later made an Indian citizen as well.)

88 (a) Uttarakhand

(Nanda Devi is 25,643 ft high. Kanchenjunga is 28,169 ft high.)

89 (c) Haryana

90 (a) @ 2500- 1,500 BCE

91 (a) Western Turkey

92 (b) Pakistan

93 (a) Kalibangan in Rajasthan

94 (b) Mound of the Dead

(This is a modern name for the city that existed thousands of years ago. The word Mohenjodaro is from Sindhi language.)

95 (a) Greek language.

(The Aryans settled initially on the banks of the river Sindhu. The Persian pronunciation of Sindhu is Hindu river (S becomes H). The Persians called the people at the river "Hindus". This Persian word became Greek Indos. So, our ancestors were called Indos people and from them the English anglicized the word Indus for the river and, the people Indians. The country name became India.

Our ancestors had called their religion Sanatana dharma. Their land as Bhaaratavarsha or Bhaarata named after the illustrious king of antiquity called Bharata, the son of Shakuntala and grandson of sage Vishvamitra. It is also described as Jambudweepa. But, there were a few kings by the name Bharata in antiquity!)

96 (b) Poros or Porus

97 (a) Only at the Jhelum region.

(Alexander's victorious army was too exhausted to advance further. They resisted and wished to return home. So, Alexander moved along the River Sindhu and thence to Babylon where he died in 323 BCE. Thus, Alexander's victory did not leave a long-lasting impact on ancient India.)

98 (b) in 185 BCE.

(This is the start of the Shunga dynasty established by Pushyamitra Shunga.)

99 (c) Odisha

100 (b) Magadha

101 (b) Rajagriha

(Later, Pataliputra became the capital, near modern Patna in Bihar.)

102 (b) Bindusara

(Note the spelling Bindusara of Mauryan dynasty. The 6th century BCE was the time of king called Bimbisara.)

103 (a) Megasthenes

(Herodotus was the famous historian. Seleucus was the Greek governor Alexander entrusted with the kingdoms he had won in India.)

104 (a) Ashoka

105 (a) Pataliputra to Takshashila.

(This is an astonishing distance of about 2,500 km long!)

106 (c) Odisha

107 (c) Near New Delhi

108 (b) Andhra Dynasty

109 (b) Maharashtra

110 (a) Chandra Gupta

(By the most amazing historical coincidence the Mauryan dynasty and the Gupta dynasty began at Magadha separated by 640 years. The founders of both dynasties are called Chandragupta. The Mauryan dynasty started around 321 BCE and the Gupta dynasty started at CE 321.)

111 (b) Vikramaditya

112 (a) Pulikeshin II

113 (b) Karnataka

(Badami is in north Karnataka and is a tourist attraction with its ancient caves and temples.)

114 (a) Afghanistan

115 (c) 17 times.

(Ghazni Mahmud raided India almost every year. He was more interested in looting the wealth and taking it than establishing himself in India, it seems.)

116 (c) CE 1024

117 (a) Prithviraj Chauhan

(In CE 1191 Prithviraj Chauhan defeated Ghuri Muhammad at Tarain. Muhammad returned the next year with a bigger army. In CE 1192 he defeated Prithviraj in the same battlefield at Tarain and captured and executed Prithviraj. This was the beginning of Muslim rule in India.)

118 (a) Qutb ud din Aibak

119 (b) Qutb ud din Aibak.

(He was a slave and became the general rising within the ranks. Ghuri Muhammad made him stay at Delhi and returned to Afghanistan. After Ghuri Muhammad died in Afghanistan, Qutb ud din Aibak established himself as Sultan of Delhi and the dynasty started. That has given the name "slave dynasty".)

120 (a) Devagiri

121 (b) Vijayanagar empire.

(This became a powerful, vast, Hindu empire in south India. It was based at what is today Hampi in north Karnataka.)

122 (a) Bahamani kingdom .

(It broke into five smaller kingdoms in CE 1347.)

123 (c) CE 1498

124 (c) Kerala

125 (b) Christopher Columbus (1451-1506)

(He was an Italian from Genoa. He was sponsored by the King and Queen of Spain and thought he could find the sea-route to India by sailing westwards from Spain. He landed in what is today Haiti and Cuba. He never visited India.

AmerigoVespucci (1454 - 1512) was an Italian merchant, navigator and sailed to the west and claimed that he had discovered the land we now call America. The continent gets the name America after his name Amerigo.)

126 (c) Alphonso de Albuquerqe

(Within 12 years of finding the sea route to India, the Portuguese captured Goa from the Sultan of Bijapur!)

127 (a) Ibrahim Lodi (Lodhi).

128 (c) Haryana

129 (a) Lion

130 (b) Humayun

131 (b) Aurangzeb

132 (b) Bahadur Shah II

(He died at the age of 87. His mother was a Rajput named Lalbai. He was defeated and imprisoned by the British and exiled into Burma (now Myanmar). He died in Rangoon jail on 7th November 1862)

133 (c) Mongol

(He had ancestry from both Mongol Chenghiz Khan and Timurlaine of Turkey. Because of his descent from the Mongol race, his dynasty was called Mughal dynasty.)

134 (c) Humayun

(He ran away to Sindh to escape the chasing Sher Shah. During this time his son and future emperor Akbar was born. After gathering military strength he came back to Delhi and defeated Sher Shah and occupied the Delhi throne once again. From CE 1526 to 1858, the Mughal empire ruled except for about fourteen years when Humayun was a fugitive! However after his recapturing Delhi, Humayun reigned about two years only and died of a fall in his palace.)

135 (a) Akbar

136 (c) Akbar

137 (a) Shah Jahan

138 (c) Akbar

139 (b) Aurangzeb

140 (c) 49 years

141 (a) Sir Thomas Roe

(He was a member of Parliament in England and acted in 1615-18 as an ambassador at Emperor Jahangir's court. Protecting the interests of the East India Company was his main work. He has written about his experiences in India and historians make use of his observations of the Indian society.)

142 (c) 14 pregnancies.

(She died at an young age of 39. She had 14 pregnancies. Aurangzeb was her son.)

143 (b) Agra Fort

144 (c) 49 years

145 (b) Akbar

(Jaziyah was a financial tax imposed on Hindus only. If a Hindu converted to Islam, he was then exempt from this tax. Thus the Jaziyah was an inducement to the Hindu to convert to Islam. Many Hindus opted and became followers of Islam. It was a form of punishment to those who remained Hindu.)

146 (a) Akbar

147 (a) Raja Todar Mal

(The finance and revenue minister. His measures were

followed for two centuries afterwards. He was a very efficient and respected minister.)

148 (a) Fatepur Sikri

149 (a) Lahore (now in Pakistan)

150 (c) Aurangzeb

151 (b) Akbar

(Babur the first Mughal emperor reigned only four years and died at the age of 47. Aurangzeb died at the age of 88 and Akbar died at the age of 63 years. Akbar ascended the throne at the age of 13 years! Both Akbar and Aurangzeb reigned 49 years. However, Akbar reigned a few months longer than Aurangzeb!)

152 (c) Shah Jahan

153 (c) Five years.

(When he ascended the throne in 1707 he was 63 year old. He reigned four years and eight months. Both Babur and Bahadur Shah have reigned for almost exactly the same duration of 4 years and 8 months.)

154 (c) Rani Jhansi Lakshmibai

(Some animals in history are famous because they were owned by a famous person! Alexander the Great in 4th century BCE had a horse that was called Bucephalus. The Buddha's horse is famous in history. (See question 205) Again, the Mughal emperor Jahangir had a pair of caged birds he had named Laila and Majnu!)

155 (b) Three times

156 (c) Yamuna (or Jamuna)

157 (c) Italy

(Marco Polo was from Venice in the 13-14th century CE. His writings of his travels in India and China have provided valuable information.)

158 (a) 15th century CE.

159 (b) 5th century CE

160 (a) 14th century CE

161 (a) Hemu (also known as Hema Chandra) was the Hindu king)

162 (a) CE 1761

163 (a) Nadir Shah

164 (a) CE 1600

165 (b) Tiger of Mysore (Mysore is in Karnataka now)

166 (c) Indore

167 (a) 29 years (1828 - June 1858)

168 (a) Meerut (now in Uttar Pradesh)

169 (b) 1858

170 (a) 1858

(Bahadur Shah II was exiled. See answer to Question 132)

171 (c) Smallpox

(This is often a fatal viral disease. Those who survive the mild disease often have scars on the skin, worse on the face cosmetically. With advances in medical science and vaccination against the virus, the disease is now eradicated.

172 (a) Krishnadevaraya

Amukta Malyada (Giver of the worn garland) is in Telugu language.

173 (c) Chief architect of the Taj Mahal at Agra

174 (b) Meerabai (CE 1498 -1557)

(She was a Hindu princess from Rajasthan. She wrote and sang bhajans, which are devotional songs in praise of the Hindu god Krishna. Her bhajans are popular all over India even today.)

175 (a) Jahangir

(She was a widow. This was her second marriage.)

176 (c) 20 years

177 (a) World Conqueror

178 (a) Shah Jahan

179 (b) Nur Jahan

(Note: all these were queens at Delhi. Mumtaz Mahal and Nur Jahan were queen consorts. Razia or Raziyya was in the 13th century CE and ruled herself as a queen of Delhi although for a short time as she was soon murdered.)

180 (a) CE 1757

(The palashi flowers in the region give the name Plassey where the battle took place. Plassey is in West Bengal.)

181 (c) Approximately 60%.

(But many more so-called independent states gave tribute to the British sovereign.)

182 (a) Tamil Nadu

183 (b) Karnataka

184 (b) Gandhar

(Takshashila university attracted students from far and wide kingdoms. The Sanskrit grammarian Panini and Chanakya the chief minister, mentor of Chandragupta Maurya were students at this university at different times.)

185 (a) Bihar

186 (a) Ujjayini

187 (c) Bombay (now Mumbai)

(Catherine of Braganza was the daughter of the king of Portugal. She married in 1662 Charles II of England. As part of the dowry, Portugal gave the city of Bombay to Charles II.)

188 (a) French

189 (c) Jaipur

190 (b) Mumbai

(They initially settled in Saurashtra and Gujarat. Later most of them moved to Bombay. They are at present fewer than 75,000 in India. Over the decades Their population is decreasing!)

191 (b) Zoroaster

192 (b) Avesta

(Zaratushtra is the founder of the Parsi religion. He is also known as Zoroaster. The Old Testament is the religious scripture of Judaism. Followers of Judaism are the Jews. Jews have migrated to India more than two thousand years ago. Their number is small but most of them settled in Cochin in Kerala and in Mumbai.)

193 (c) Buddhism

194 (c) Siddhartha.

(Devadatta was Siddhartha's cousin. Maitreya Buddha is a

Bodhisatva and, according to Buddhist belief, he will be born in the future to teach dharma.)

195 (a) Bimbisara

196 (a) Vihar

(In ancient times many vihars were built. The area they were predominantly built became known as Bihar.)

197 (b) Yashodhara

(Maya Devi was the Buddha's mother. Amrapali was a famous courtesan and contemporary of the Buddha.)

198 (b) Rahul

(Anand was the Buddha's favourite disciple. He was also the Buddha's cousin.)

199 (a) Pure or genuine.

(The fully initiated Sikhs belong to the Khalsa.)

200 (c) Fire temple of Parsees

(The Parsis worship fire. It is said when they migrated to India from Persia, they brought with them the sacred fire which is continuing to burn until now.)

201 (a) Magadhi

(Sanskrit was the language of the learned. To reach the masses, the Buddha chose Magadhi language which most people could understand.)

202 (c) 49 days

203 (b) 30 years

204 (b) Nepal

205 (c) Kanthaka

206 (c) Kandy (Sri Lanka)

207 (a) Sarnath (Near Varanasi, Uttar Pradesh)

208 (c) the Rig Veda -- @ 1400 BCE

209 (a) Mahavira

210 (c) St. Thomas

211 (c) Shankaracharya

212 (a) Buddhism

(The schism occurred after the death of the Buddha.)

213 (c) Jataka stories

214 (c) the Rig Veda

215 (b) Jainism

216 (a) Patanjali

217 (b) Tirthankara

(In all there were 24 Tirthankaras. Mahavira is the 24th. The first Tirhankara was Rishabhanatha.)

218 (b) Shankaracharya

219 (a) submit to God

220 (a) Recital

(It is word of God dictated to the Prophet, which is recited and read.)

221 (a) Channa

222 (a) Kushinagar (now in Uttar Pradesh)

223 (b) Gaya (in Bihar)

224 (a) Shakya

(The Buddha is also called Shakyamuni because of his origin.)

225 (a) Vaishali (in modern Bihar)

(A few other places have claimed the same as Vaishali.)

226 (c) Vardhamana

227 (b) 12 years

228 (c) Nashik

229 (a) Himachal Pradesh

230 (a) Basaveshvara

(In the Indian cultural and religious history Basaveshvara stands as a great revolutionary. He fought against the religious rituals and caste system and made social reforms. He was the minister of the Jain king Bijjala at Kalyan in Karnataka. He also wrote innumerable 'vachana' which are full of moralistic and religious thoughts. In Kannada language, vachana sahitya is a great literary achievement of the 12th century.)

231 (c) Akbar

232 (c) Maharashtra.

(His devotional songs are very popular and are known as abhanga)

233 (a) Karnataka

(He was a vaishnava and devotee of Vithal (Vishnu). His devotional, moralistic songs are very popular in Karnataka. His contemporary Kanakadasa has also enriched the Kannada literature with his equally popular devotional songs.)

234 (b) Guru Nanak

235 (b) Guru Gobindsingh

236 (a) Guru Arjan the fifth Guru.

237 (a) Guru Gobindsingh, the tenth Guru

238 (c) Guru Arjan. In the 16th century

239 (b) Ten

240 (b) Dayananda Saraswati

241 (a) Raja Ram Mohan Roy

242 (b) Place of Prayer and Prostration

243 (b) Chicago

244 (c) Robert Clive

245 (a) William Bentinck

(Earlier the language of palace and court was Persian.)

246 (c) Raja Gulabsingh

247 (b) Warren Hastings (1772 - 1785)

248 (a) Lord Canning in 1858

249 (c) Lord Curzon

250 (a) General Dyer

In the Jalianwala Bagh in Amritsar a peaceful crowd was subjected to firing by the British Army on the orders of Brigadier – General Dyer. Hundreds of innocent children, women and men died. Some sources have claimed about one thousand people died. This tragic event happened on 13 April 1919.

251 (c) Dadabhoy Naoroji

(He was the first Asian MP to be elected to the British Parliament. He was elected in 1892 from Finsbury, a London borough, and represented the Liberal party.)

252 (a) 1885

253 (c) Dadabhoy Naoroji

254 (a) 1912

(Before that Calcutta was the administrative capital of British India.)

255 (a) 1911

256 (b) Dadabhoy Naoroji

257 (c) Rabindranath Tagore

258 (b) 1906

259 (b) Gopal Krishna Gokhale

260 (b) Lokamanya Tilak

(Bal Gangadhar Tilak was called Lokamanya – respected throughout the World.)

261 (a) 1931

262 (b) Vallabhbhai Patel

263 (a) Subhas Chandra Bose

264 (b) Sarojini Naidu

265 (a) Bihar

266 (b) Vallabhbhai Patel

267 (b) 1942

268 (c) Dandi.

(A village on the seashore of Gujarat.)

269 (b) Lokamanya Tilak (This is in Marathi.)

270 (b) Khan Abdul Gafar Khan

271 (c) Lokamanya Tilak

272 (b) Lokamanya Tilak

273 (b) Shimla

274 (c) 7 years

(Mahatma Gandhi was jailed a few times. However, the time he spent in jail was reduced at times with release earlier than the sentence given by the courts. He lived 78 years but spent about seven years in imprisonment!)

275 (c) about a million

276 (c) 75,000

(And many more were injured!)

277 (c) Two millions.

(The situation of the famine was mismanaged by the central government that led to this great human loss. When the Japanese occupied Burma (Myanmar) the supply of food to India was scarce. The British Government in Delhi did not act soon enough to redistribute the available food, which led to avoidable deaths.)

278 (c) 2.5 million

(The Indian Army was the largest voluntary army to help the British in the Second World War. About 85,000 recorded as dead or missing and about 60,000 were in captivity.Thirty Indian soldiers received the Victoria Cross award.)

279 (b) Clement Attlee

(He was Labour Party leader and Prime Minister.)

280 (b) George VI

(He was the father of Queen Elizabeth II, the present monarch of Britain.)

281 (b) Punjab – Afghan - Kashmir- Sindh

282 (c) 560 approximately

(Some were very small estates. Some were large, such as

Hyderabad, Mysore.)

283 (a) Lord Mountbatten

284 (a) Rajendra Prasad

285 (a) C. Rajagopalachari

(Also known as Chakravarti Rajagopalachariar and Rajaji.)

286 (a) Sarojini Naidu (Governor of Uttar Pradesh)

(Her daughter Padmaja Naidu became the Governor of West Bengal in 1961.)

287 (c) 17 years

(Uninterrupted from 15 August 1947 to 27 May 1964 – the day he died. Approximately seventeen years of his term in office is the longest as Prime Minister so far in India)

288 (b) Rajkumari Amrit Kaur (Cabinet Minister for Health)

289 (a) S. Radhakrishnan

290 (c) C. Rajagopalachari

(The post was abolished and the post of President of India was created in 1950.)

291 (a) Sucheta Kripalani (Chief Minister of Uttar Pradesh 1963-1967)

292 (c) Vinoba Bhave

293 (c) Lal Bahadur Shastri

294 (a) Bankim Chandra Chatterjee

295 (a) K.M. Cariappa (from Kodagu in Karnataka)

296 (a) Mohammed Ali Jinnah

297 (a) S. Radhakrishnan

298 (c) Gen K.M.Cariappa

299 (b) 1950 (26th January)

300 (c) 1971

301 (b) Rabindranath Tagore

302 (c) 1961

(Although India became independent on 15th August 1947, Goa remained under the control of the Portuguese. In 1961 during the premiership of Jawaharlal Nehru, the Portuguese occupation of Goa was forcibly ended.)

303 (a) Vijayalakshmi Pandit

304 (c) Chief Justice of India

305 (c) B.R.Ambedkar

306 (b) the President of India

307 (b) 1971

(During the premiership of Indira Gandhi the Indian Parliament passed a motion to end the privilege of Privy Purse .)

308 (b) Lal Bahadur Shastri (2nd October 1904)

309 (c) S. Radhakrishnan

(He was a professor of philosophy. He was born on 5th September 1888. In honour of him, his birthday is celebrated as Teachers' Day.)

310 (a) Sarojini Naidu

(She was a celebrated poet. "Golden Threshold" is the collection of her poems)

311 (a) Jayaprakash Narayan

312 (b) Lal Bahadur Shastri

(This was at the time of Indo-Pakistan war of 1965. To combat the enemy at the border and to enthuse the farmer to work harder to meet the needs of the nation.)

313 (c) Indira Gandhi

314 (c) 1962

315 (a) This war lasted a month and China was victorious.

316 (c) Kashmir (It is the north-east region of Kashmir.)
317 (b) Four Indo-Pak wars have been fought.
(These wars occurred in 1947, 1965, 1971 and 1999. India

has won all the wars with Pakistan. In 1971, India helped the liberation of East Pakistan, which became the independent Bangladesh. The last war was the Kargil war in 1999.)

318 (b) India and Pakistan

(Following the Indo-Pak war of 1965, a peace conference was held at Tashkent (now capital of independent Uzbekistan) with the Russian mediation. Indian Prime Minister Lal Bahadur Shastri and the Pakistan President Ayub Khan signed the peace agreement. Tragically, Lal Bahdur Shastri died at Tashkent on 11 January 1966. He is the only Indian Prime Minister to have died abroad.)

319 (a) 25 years

320 (b) 30

321 (b) 35

322 (a) 25 years.

(As an MP of Lok Sabha it is 25 years. As a member of Rajya Sabha it is 30 years. Interestingly, during the British rule of India, in 1783 William Pitt the younger became the Prime Minister of Britain at the age of 24 and held that position for17 years!)

323 (c) 54 countries

324 (c) London
325 (c) Vijayalakshmi Pandit

326 (a) Madras (now Chennai)

327 (b) Allahabad

(So far, more Prime Ministers are from Allahabad. Their constituencies have been around there. Some are associated with the institutions in Allahabad in their career. This has given the name to Allahabad as the city of Prime Ministers.)

328 (a) Guru Ramdas

329 (a) CE 736

330 (b) Allahabad

(Prayag is an ancient holy city of the Hindus. Prayag , meaning "Place of Offerings", is at the confluence of three rivers Ganga, Yamuna and the mythical Saraswati. Its name was changed in the Mughal time.)

331 (b) Pune

(in Maharashtra. Previously anglicized as Poona.)

332 (a) Ayodhya.

333 (a) New Delhi

334 (a) Chandigarh

335 (a) 1931
336 (c) Mumbai

337 (a) Madras (now Chennai)

338 (c) 1971

339 (a) Odisha

340 (a) Rajasthan

341 (b) Kanyakumari

342 (b) Ellora

343 (a) Angkor Wat in Cambodia

344 (a) Jaipur

345 (b) Raipur

(The capital of Chhattisgarh. Swami Vivekananda spent some time in this town in his earlier days.)

346 (c) Hyderabad

347 (b) Mahatma Gandhi

348 (c) Mumbai

349 (a) Sarnath (in Uttar Pradesh)

350 (c) 84 thousand.

351 (b) Rashtrakuta king
352 (c) Hyderabad

353 (a) Panini

(This book contains about 4000 grammar rules in eight sections.)

354 (b) Physician

355 (b) Sushruta

(His famous book is Sushruta samhita.)

356 (c) Uttarakhand

357 (b) Kautilya (also spelt Kautalya. His name was Vishnugupta.)

(He was the mentor of Chandragupta and a strategist in removing the Nanda king and helping Chandragupta in establishing the Mauryan Dynasty in @ 321 BCE.)

358 (a) Valmiki

359 (a) Bhagavadgita. It was translated into English and published in 1785.

360 (b) Vyasamaharshi

(The Mahabharata has about 100,000 stanzas. It is longer than the Greek epics the Iliad and the Odyssey combined!)

361 (c) Pali

362 (b) Camp

(In the Mughal time the army soldiers were Turkish, Persian, Hindus, Afghans and during the camping they needed a communication language. The language developed in the camps, Urdu, means "camp". So the language came to be called Urdu language or Urdu.)

363 (c) Jawaharlal Nehru

(Glimpses of World History is another seminal work by Nehru which he wrote whilst he was in jail. Both these books have attained classics status.)

364 (b) Ibn Battuta

365 (b) Tamil

366 (b) Valmiki

367 (a) James Prinsep

(He was a British officer in Calcutta. He was the first person to decipher the ancient Brahmi script and also able to read the edicts of the Mauryan Emperor Ashoka. This made a great progress in understanding the history of India.)

368 (a) Ardhamagadhi

369 (c) Kannada

370 (a) Kalidasa

371 (c) Devanagari

372 (b) Panchatantra

(This was a collection of animal stories to teach the statecraft to the not so intelligent three princes. Note Vishnugupta is the name of the famous Kautilya and he wrote Arthashastra a treatise on polity.)

373 (b) Sanskrit

374 (b) Kashmir

375 (b) Tamil

376 (a) Harsha (CE 594 – 647)

377 (a) Tamil

378 (b) Vishakhadatta

(This is a famous play about Chanakya, Chandragupta and Amatya Rakshasa, and political intrigue.)

379 (b) Tamil

380 (b) Tulasidas

381 (b) Kerala

382 (c) Kabirdas

383 (b) Bhimbetka caves (near Bhopal, Madhya Pradesh)

384 (c) Maharashtra

385 (c) Kamakshi temple

386 (a) Karnataka

387 (c) Bahubali

388 (c) 238 feet

389 (b) 57 feet.

(This was erected in late 10th century CE and is carved in a huge single stone. There are a few taller statues in India but they are not carved of a single stone. Every twelve years the Bahubali statue is subjected to the spectacular mahama-stakaabhisheka celebration of pouring milk on his head. Thousands of people from all over India attend the ceremony.)

390 (a) Burial mounds of the Buddhist saints

391 (c) Madura

392 (b) A huge rock elephant was discovered on this island
.

393 (b) Mumbai

(Overlooking the Arabian sea to the west, this magnificent architectural structure is one of the famous landmarks of Mumbai.)

394 (c) New Delhi

395 (a) C.V.Raman

(In the first year three were awarded this honour. The other two are Dr S. Radhakrishnan and C. Rajagopalachari)

396 (b) Mathematics

397 (b) Victoria Cross Medal

(The Victoria Cross is awarded to a person who has shown extreme courage . This is named after the British Queen Victoria and was instituted in 1860s. Khudadad Khan, Gabar Singh Negi and Dawar Singh Negi became the first three Indians to receive this medal in 1914 for their courageous fighting in the First World War.)

398 (a) G. Shankar Kurup . Malayalam poet

(For his anthology Odakkuzhal, (the bamboo flute). Gujarati poet Umashankar Joshi and Kannada poet D.R. Bendre were also the recipients of this award but in later years.)

399 (a) Rabindranath Tagore.

(His famous work is Gitanjali – offering of songs – which was awarded the Nobel prize for literature in 1913. He became the first Asian to win the Nobel Prize.)

400 (b) Arundhati Roy
(in 1997, for her novel God of Small Things)

(The prize is called the Man Booker prize but is popularly known as Booker Prize.)

401 (a) Rabindranath Tagore

(C.P.Ramaswamy Iyer renounced his knighthood
soon after India became independent.)

402 (a) Queen Victoria.

(She was also made the Empress of India in 1877.)

403 (c) Vinoba Bhave

404 (c) Devika Rani (actress)

405 (b) Rudyard Kipling (in 1907)

(Poets W.B.Yeats and T.S. Eliot
are also Nobel Prize winners.)

406 (b) M.S.Subbulakshmi
(distinguished Carnatic music singer)

407 (c) Gwalior (Madhya Pradesh)

(Hindus were the first to use zero as a digit. They also
invented the now universally used decimal system. In the
decimal notation the value of the digit is related to its
position in a given number. The Arabs learnt these from the
Hindus, and through the Arabs it went to European
countries. It is described as the Arab-Hindu system.)

408 (c) Aryabhata (also spelt Aryabhatta)

(A great mathematician and astronomer, CE 476- 550. He
was the first to use letters to represent numbers in
mathematical calculations. He wrote his famous work
Aryabhatiya at the very young age of 23, in CE 499.)

409 (a) Jaipur

(Also. the city of Jaipur is named after him)

410 (a) C.V. Raman

(He was awarded the Nobel prize for physics in 1930 for his discovery of what is known as the 'Raman Effect'. He is the first Asian scientist to win the Nobel Prize in science. The Indian born Hargobind Khorana won the Nobel prize for medicine and physiology. He became a naturalized American – as did C. Subrahmanyan who won the Nobel prize for physics in 1983. C. Subrahmanyan was born in Lahore, now in Pakistan. He was the nephew of C.V. Raman, who was Nobel Prize winner 53 years earlier.)

411 (b) boson

(All matter is made up of small atoms. Atoms are invisible but scientists have discovered their internal structure by experiments and mathematical calculations. Such particles are called subatomic particles. Scientists have discovered dozens of subatomic particles and depending on their behavior and properties they are called bosons or fermions. The descriptive term boson is named in honour of the Indian physicist Satyen Bose. The other name fermion is in honour of the physicist Enrico Fermi.)

412 (c) Vaisheshika

(In ancient Hindu philosophy six schools of thought were recognized. The Vaisheshika school believed that all matter is made of small particles called 'paramanu'. This resembles the modern scientific thought of structure of the matter.)

413 (a) Guntur in Andhra Pradesh

(The second lightest element is helium. It was discovered for the first time by spectroscopic observations. The discovery of that element in the Sun during a solar eclipse gave its name helium as helios in Greek mythology is the Sun. More than ten years later the same element was for the first time discovered on the earth! The observational experiments were conducted in Guntur during a solar eclipse in the 19th century. Similar simultaneous experiment was conducted in Maharashtra.)

414 (c) 1974

415 (c) Bengaluru

416 (b) Vikram Sarabhai

417 (a) Satyen Bose

(called Bose-Einstein statistics)

418 (a) J.B.S.Haldane

(He was a pioneering scientist in genetics and biology. He protested against the British involvement in the Suez crisis and became an Indian citizen. He died in Bhuvaneshvar in Odisha.)

419 (b) Jagadish Chandra Bose

(Meghanad Saha was a physicist renowned for his discoveries of star temperature and colour of the stars and many more pioneering works. Prafulla Chandra Ray was an acclaimed chemist and he is credited as the Father of Modern Indian Chemistry.)

420 (b) daughter

(Bhaskara II CE 1114-1193. He is called Bhaskaracharya and also Bhaskara II to distinguish him from another famous mathematician of the same name a few centuries earlier. Bhaskaracharya wrote Siddhantashiromani at the age of 36. Lilavati is the arithmetic part of this work. This he has written addressing questions to Lilavati, who was his unmarried daughter. The legend has it that the young girl failed to marry due to her ill-stars! To console her Bhaskaracharya wrote this book. Whatever the reason, the mathematics of Bhaskaracharya are a great achievement of the 12th century.)

421 (b) Mathematics

422 (b) Ronald Ross

(He identified the parasite responsible for causing Malaria and also determined the mode of transmission as being through mosquitoes. This was a great discovery because then, the disease was thought to be spread by bad air around the swamps. The name of the disease malaria is from Italian. mala = bad + aria = air . Ronald Ross won the Nobel Prize in 1902.)

423 (b) Asiatic Society

(This was established in Calcutta. William Jones was a British judge. The establishment of the Asiatic Society led to the western scholars studying of Hindu Sanskrit works of antiquity and understanding Hindu culture, religion and literature. Soon, many Sanskrit texts were translated into English.)

424 (b) Bangalore Torpedo

425 (a) Rajasthan

426 (a) Kerala

(Thumba is a suburban part of the city of Thiruvan-anthpuram)

427 (a) Aryabhata

(Named in honour of the famous 5th century mathematician and astronomer, Aryabhata.)

428 (b) Soviet Union Cosmodrome

429 (c) Bengaluru

430 (a) Rakesh Sharma

(Ravish Malhotra also trained as a cosmonaut and as a stand-by. But Rakesh Sharma was successful in training and being the first Indian space traveller. Kalpana Chawla was a born Indian but was a naturalized American and was an American astronaut. Most horrifyingly she died in the Columbia disaster along with her companion astronauts.)

431 (b) Bengaluru

432 (a) Sriharikota

(This is a small island in the Bay of Bengal, east of Andhra Pradesh.)

433 (c) Mumbai

(In Trombay near Mumbai. It is named in honour of the Indian physicist Homi J. Bhabha.)

434 (a) Sriharikota

435 (a) Three
(USA, Russia and China)

436 (a) Commercial Airlines in India in the 1930s.

437 (c) 65,000 km

(This is the length of the routes across India. But there are several lines on these routes making the length of the rail lines much more. Interestingly for comparison the circumference of the Earth at the equator is about 40,000 km.)

438 (a) Mercury

(Craters are circular or oval sometimes incomplete depressions on the surface of a planet. Mercury has thousands of such craters of varying diameters. The International Astronomical Union is the official body that names such features on the planets.)

439 (b) Venus

(The second planet nearest to the Sun is Venus. Hindus call this as Shukra. However, in western astronomy the planet is a female. Venus is the Roman goddess of love and beauty. It is the same as Greek goddess of love and beauty, Aphrodite. International Astronomical Union decided to name all features on the planet Venus only by female names. One or two rare exceptions have occurred. Lakshmi planum is named after the Hindu goddess Lakshmi. It is a plateau about two and a half mile high.By comparison, Mt Everest, the the highest peak on Earth, is 5.5 miles high.)

440 (a) Raja Harishchandra

(Dadasaheb Phalke was the producer and director of this silent film. This was released in 1913. This was the story of Harishchandra's promise to the sage Vishvamitra which led to the tragedy of abandoning his wife Taramati.)

441 (a) Alam Ara

(Alam Ara meaning Ornament of the World. This was directed by Ardeshir Irani. Zubeida and Prithviraj Kapoor were the lead heroine and hero. The story is from the Parsi literature.)

442 (b) Hyderabad

(Ramoji Film City is the world's largest integrated film city.)

443 (c) Mumbai

444 (c) Kerala

445 (b) Painter

446 (a) Bharatamuni

447 (c) Kerala

(Mohiniattam is also another classical Indian dance that originated in Kerala.)

448 (a) Andhra Pradesh (Kuchipudi is the village)

449 (a) Carnatic (variant spelling is Karnatak)

450 (b) Percussion instrument

451 (a) Languages

452 (c) Nagaland

453 (c) Rudyard Kipling

454 (b) Chindits

(The Chindits mainly fought the Japanese in Burma, now called Myanmar.)

455 (a) Dum Dum

(The English word 'dolally' means becoming crazy or losing one's mind. This English word is corruption of the name of the village deolali near Mumbai. Here the British had an army transit camp.)

456 (a) 15%

(Although the British established many educational institutions in India, overall they did not make the country literate. Most of the leap in literacy in India has been since independence. Today the literacy rate of India is about 65% which is a great progress.)

457 (a) Doctor of Medicine

(As she was denied admission to medical college in India, she travelled to America and qualified as a doctor from Pennsylvania. She returned to India as a doctor and worked only a short time in Kolhapur, which is in Maharashtra now. Tragically she died at a very young age of 22 from tuberculosis. In the same year as Anandi Joshi, another Indian woman Kadambini Ganguly also qualified as a doctor. Surely they paved the way for other Indian women to pursue a career in medicine.)

458 (a) Pingali Venkayya

(He was a designer and artist from Andhra Pradesh.)

459 (c) 24

460 (a) barrister.

(She studied and qualified as a barrister in England.)

461 (c) All of them

(Sanskrit sharkara = sugar. Karsh was Sanskrit word for ancient Indian coin that has given rise to the English word cash for money. Sanskrit word khandasharkara = candy, the gemstone upala = opal, visha (Sanskrit) = virus, another gemstone in Sanskrit vaidhurya = beryl, bandicoot is derived from Telugu words pandi + kokku = pig rat, juggernaut is a word for huge lorries and machineries and is from the famous huge chariot at the temple of Jagannathpuri. Shampoo is from Hindi.)

462 (c) 20

463 (b) Jodhpuris

(Horse jockeys, polo players and hunters wear jodhpuris.)

464 (b) 1901

465 (c) Kerala

466 (c) Mysore

(Completed in 1861, this palace in Mysore, Karnataka, has wonderful collections of paintings by Raja Ravi Varma and many other Indian painters.)

467 (a) Vishakhapattanam (Andhra Pradesh)

468 (c) A type of fish (believe it or not!)

469 (c) Tea

470 (a) 1881

471 (c) Peacock (peafowl)

472 (a) Lotus

473 (b) Calicut (in Kerala)

474 (c) Kolkata

475 (b) Tiger

476 (c) Mango

477 (a) Karnataka

478 (a) Mountain of Light

479 (a) Bombay - Thane

(This is about 30 kilometres distance. See the answer to Question 437.)

480 (c) Kolkata

481 (b) Uttarakhand

482 (c) Kanyakumari to Varanasi (Benares)

483 (a) New York Philharmonic Orchestra

484 (c) Kolkata

485 (a) Mihir Sen (in 1958)

(Arati Saha was the first Indian woman to achieve that feat, in 1959. Dolly Nazir was an accomplished Olympic swimmer of India.)

486 (a) 1792

487 (b) Kerala

488 (c) Snooker

489 (a) C.K.Nayadu

490 (a) Tamil

491 (b) Auction bridge

492 (b) Manipur

493 (a) Chess

494 (b) Indian Ocean

(The sea at the south of India. When Europeans had to come to India by the sea route they had to cross this mass of water and the name came because of the geographical association of India with this sea. The chemical element Indium, 49th on the periodic table, is named after an indigo colour spectral line this element produces. It is not named after India. However, indigo colour itself got the name from a dye that was extensively produced by India from a very long time. Indian summer is nothing related to India. It is a late autumn warm weather in America and is the time when American Indians go away to enjoy this warm weather!)

495 (a) Albert Einstein

496 (b) Group

(This group consists of finance ministers and directors of

the central banks of the top 20 economically advanced nations.)

497 (c) Bhopal

(This incident of chemical leakage and death of nearly 4000 people in their sleep shocked the world. It is the worst disaster of its kind in the world.)

498 (a) New Delhi

(Considering the number of passengers this is the biggest. India has 11 International Airports and a total of about 125 airports that includes domestic passenger airports, military and defence airports.)

499 (b) Mundaka Upanishad

500 (c) Prime Minister of India

(This is the official residence of the Prime minister of India since 1984.)

501 (c) Albert Einstein

STATES OF INDIA

Daman & Diu

Dadra & nagar
Haveli

Lakshadweep islands

Andaman &
Nicobar islands

1. Kerala (Thiruvananthapuram) 2. Tamil Nadu (Chennai)
3. Andhra Pradesh (Hyderabad) 4. Karnataka (Bengaluru) 5. Goa
(Panji) 6. Maharashtra (Mumbai) 7. Telangana (Hyderabad)
8. Chhattis-garh (Raipur) 9. Odisha (Bhuvaneshwar) 10. West
Bengal (Kolkata) 11. Sikkim (Gangtok) 12. Bihar (Patna)
13. Jharkhand (Ranchi) 14. Uttar Pradesh (Lucknow) 15. Madhya
Pradesh (Bhopal) 16 Gujarat (Gandhinagar) 17. Rajasthan
(Jaipur) 18. Haryana (Chadingarh) 19. Punjab (Chandigarh)
20. Uttarakhand (Dehradun) 21. Himachal Pradesh (Shimla)
22. Jammu & Kashmir (Shrinagar) 23. Arunachal Pradesh
(Itanagar) 24. Nagaland (Kohima) 25. Manipur (Imphal)
26. Mizoram (Aizawl) 27 Tripura (Agartala) 28. Meghalaya
(Shillong) 29. Assam (Dispur)

IMPORTANT PLACES

RIVERS OF INDIA

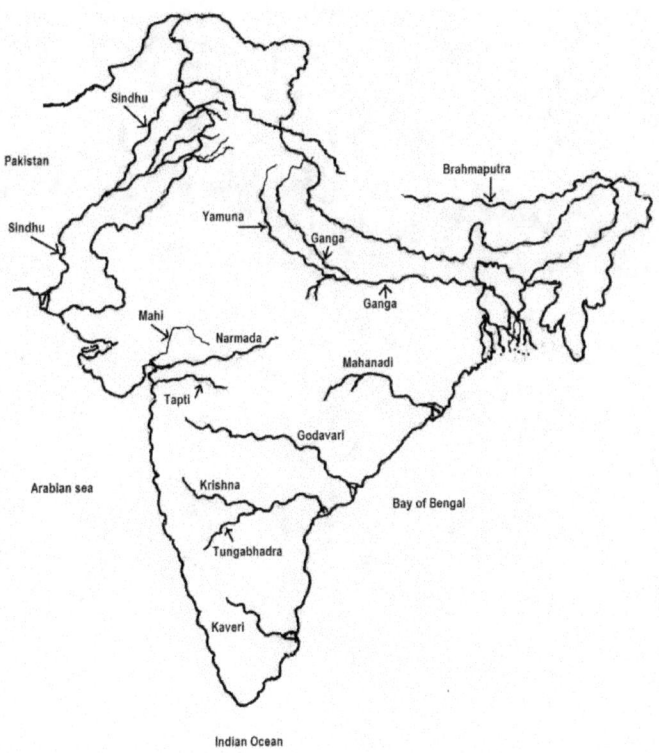

www.ingramcontent.com/pod-product-compliance
Lightning Source LLC
Chambersburg PA
CBHW060627290526
45793CB00001B/176